Robin Hood
The Spirit of the Forest

Robin Hood
The Spirit of the Forest

by

Steve Wilson

Neptune Press
49a Museum Street, London WC1A 1LY

ISBN 0 9505001 5 1

**Front cover illustration
by
Jo Strevens-Weir**

Made and printed in Great Britain by Booksprint, Bristol, England

DEDICATION

THIS book is dedicated to the Oxleas Nine, whose
fight continues, and to Terry and Jere Baker, Nigel
Bourne and Seldiy Bates, Debbie Benstead and Andrew
Collins, Karl Duncan, Boyd Lees, Chrys Livings, Hal
Hartzell Jr., Johnny Merron, Alan Moore, Steve Moore,
The Manager of the Bugle Horn, Charlton, Nigel
Pennick, Chesca Potter, Spirit Of Sherwood magazine,
Olivia Robertson and Lawrence Durdin-Robertson,
Phillip Shallcross, Mark Ryan and Caroline Wise.

Robin Hood
The Spirit of the Forest

STEVE WILSON became interested in mythology as a child at boading school. This interest developed whilst studying at Dulwich College. He began investigating Eastern mysticism in 1967 and the Western mysteries in the 1970s. He received an Honours Degree in Religion and Philosophy from what is now Middlesex University in 1986. A member of the *Fellowship of Isis* since 1981, he was ordained as a Priest in the Fellowship in 1984. With Vivien O'Reagan, he founded the first Fellowship of Isis Lyceum, outside the foundation temple in Eire, in 1986. He currently edits *Aisling*, the magazine of the Druid Clan of Dana (a daughter organisation of the FOI) and represents the *Council of British Druid Orders* on the Pagan Federation Council. He also chairs the weekly *Philosoforum* discussion group in Greenwich and *Talking Stick*, the fortnightly meeting held in Central London. The contents of this book were first presented at the *Robin Hood and the Green Man* conference at Charlton in April 1992.

CONTENTS

OLD MAY-DAY.

KING HENRY VIII. AT SHOOTER'S HILL.

FOREWORD

AS a writer of fiction; as someone for whom the writing of fiction is at once sole source of livelihood and sole practiced magical discipline, I have obviously given the matter of story-telling more than a little thought over the last fifteen years. I have attempted to define, at least to my own satisfaction, the nature of the animal: its anatomy, its motivations and the way in which it functions in the world. As someone who believes that it is better to travel hopefully than to arrive, I am pleased to say that as yet I have reached absolutely no conclusions, although I have encountered some interesting notions and systems of thought as landmarks and landscape along the way.

One idea that continues to fascinate me is that upon a deep, virtual level, fiction is a more honest form of truth. Our allegedly "true" histories, both cultural and personal, begin to perspire and shift uncomfortably when exposed to the bright, third-degree lights of any strenuous interrogation.

On a cultural level, our model of History seems only to approach anything resembling accuracy when it deals with the broadest generalities. We have identified and labelled certain periods in our view of human development according to what our culture perceives as the dominant characteristics of those periods. Thus, we can say with some certainty that the Paleolithic era preceded Neolithic times, and that these were followed by the Bronze and Iron Ages respectively. This statement is undeniably true, yet since it only describes a human system of labelling and identification, it might be argued that it is no more intrinsically valuable than the statement that "B" precedes "C" in our alphabet, followed by "D" and "E" respectively.

When History attempts a more detailed and specialized analysis of the past, its limitations become more evident. Even when pertaining to events within living memory such as the Kennedy assassination or the Vietnam war, the constant stream of fresh disclosures on both subjects would indicate that the officially accepted tapestry of our past has some clumsy tucks here and there, a few gaping holes and a general appearance of having been badly stitched up.

Predictably, when History (a highly localised science) attempts to present a realistic picture of events more remote in time, the fabric becomes even more dilapidated and untrustworthy. Two separate dynasties of Egyptian Pharaohs will suddenly collapse into one, due to an error in our dating systems or a misreading of the evidence. A mysterious two-century period from which no cultural artefacts have been unearthed, supposed to have been a cataclysmic and cultureless "Dark Age", will stand revealed as a mirage brought on by faulty mathematics; two hundred years that simply never existed save as an archeological delusion.

Pushed to the boundaries and made to account for the origins of life, our tapestry begins more to resemble a vast and monstrously complicated jigsaw, begun then left abandoned in either boredom or frustration: Darwin has found one or two of the corner pieces and has completed one of the straight edges, while over on the other side of the table the major world religions have patiently picked out all of the light blue pieces that look like they might be sky, yet still the centre is a yawning void.

Pressed further, to the limits of existence itself, History merges with Physics. Above the squabbling of the physicists as they debate their various theories as to our material origins, the digitized and emblematically modern voice of Steven Hawking confesses that he is unwilling to entirely exclude the possibility of a Creator from his equations. At its furthest extremity, our tapestry is reduced to a few bare and solitary threads of speculation that reach only a little way into the fathomless dark beyond. Each thread, each system of belief has its own integrity and value and yet, in the final analysis, it is *only* that: a system of belief.

The problem arises with our human tendency to confuse map and territory. Tentative models of existence grow into monolithic and petrified dogmas; massive structures that block the path of our thinking, that hinder our development and can only be removed by the application of dynamite. Perhaps all our models of History and existence should bear the mental health equivalent of the Government warnings found on cigarette packaging? Perhaps, the Zen candour of Magritte's "Ceci n'est pas une pipe", all our representations of the Universe should bear the legend "Ceci n'est pas un Universe"?

Which returns us to fiction; to myth and to legend; the only form of historical information that clearly bears such a warning. By proclaiming themselves to be fictions, myth and legend achieve what is to my mind almost a superior level of truth and honesty. History, written by victors, may present

Richard III to us as a malignant hunchback and unworthy ruler, but that is merely an interpretation and as such is subject to challenge and revision. As information, its value is debatable.

Shakespeare's play of that title, on the other hand, offers us a more certain truth: We may be sure that while the scenes and events within the drama do not profess to be accurate reconstructions of reality, they at least tell us that the ideas and notions contained within those scenes were valued and cherished by the people of the day. They tell us something about how they thought; about the evolving landscape of the human mind, the shadow-territory wherein lies the source of all the human advances and events that go to make up our "actual" History.

Given that events in the past no longer have any actual existence, their cataloguing can surely have no greater claim to be objective truth, no useful information content that is superior in value to our legends of Achilles and Hector, of Arthur, or of Robin Hood? Events in the past, whether self-confessedly mythical or allegedly "real" are simply apparent lighted points of information in the firmament of our consciousness. While we can no more reach out across time and establish the "truth" of those lighted points than we can reach out across space to prod the stars, they have a value in that we can draw lines between the points and link them up into metaphysical constellations; systems that enable us to navigate. In this context, in this firmament, the stars of myth and history are of equal value, and shine equally as bright.

This is the territory of the para- or psycho-historians, those who examine and dissect the dusty artefacts of fable with as much care and applied insight as conventional history brings to the painstaking reconstruction of an archeological excavation. In a very real sense, this is not "soft" history; not merely a kind of elaborate mind-game indulged on the fringes of conventional research. It is important and hard and vital if we are to understand our own thinking, the very source of all historical triumphs and cataclysms.

It is therefore particularly enjoyable to come across a book like Steve Wilson's "Robin Hood - The Spirit of the Forest". In this fascinating work, the erudition of which does not over-reach its ability to engage, Wilson takes one of our foremost national myth-figures and subjects that myth to a rigourous anatomical analysis, taking nothing for granted and leaving no ventricle unprobed, unearthing in the process a treasure-house of facts and ideas which he then connects skilfully by means of trenchant and intelligent observation into a compelling and revealing thesis.

Leaving the chimera of an "historical" Robin Hood for the more pedantic and hidebound explorers, Wilson plunges instead into the very roots of the legend, sweeping engagingly through the many parallels to be found in Indian mythology and suggesting a possible Neolithic origin for this enduring tale of near-superhuman archers that hide within the greenwood.

Not content with simply examining the birth-process of a mythic archetype, the author seems also concerned with the growth and evolution of this creature. He examines the many forms that it has taken across the span of its unearthly metaphysical life, along with the many appendages that it has either grown or had grafted on to it, from Robin Hood as avatar of Odin to Robin Hood as a priapic symbol of fertility. Every element of the legend is identified, examined and extrapolated upon, from the associated myth of the Bad King to a rumination upon the symbolism of the longbow.

Given his evident erudition and the depth of research, it is gratifying to note that Wilson has avoided any hint of cultural snobbery. Recognizing that in commercial television and mass pulp literature there exists a strong link with the ballads, broadsheets and oral traditions of old, Wilson extends his examination of the myth into the present day, finding as much of interest in television series such as "Robin of Sherwood" or films such as "Robin and Marion" as he does in pre-Christian epics such as the Ramayana.

This is a remarkable work, sober and penetrating while remaining eminently readable at all times. Mapping the firmament of ideas, Steve Wilson has provided us with a superb sky-chart, as reliable as it is revelatory. His arrow is straight and his aim is true. Read, learn and enjoy.

Alan Moore
Northampton, February 1993

INTRODUCTION

I WAS born in the 20th Century and was brought up to speak English. This means that like countless millions I know about Robin Hood. From childhood story-books through early television series to the films, cartoons and finally the mystical TV series 'Robin Of Sherwood' it is almost impossible not to have heard of him, as well as Maid Marian, the Merry Men, the Sheriff, Guy of Gisborn and all the rest. I have also read the many interpretations of the legend, ranging from historical enquiries to esoteric whimsy. Fascinating though these were, however, it was not until I visited India in 1981 that I ever suspected that Robin might be older than the tales suggest. As we shall see in Chapter Two, Robin may be very old indeed.

Most of the debate about Robin used to be based upon historical developments. As a boy I read of the possibility that robber bands of dispossessed Saxons inspired the legends, fighting a guerrilla war against the Norman overlords, that Robin was probably based upon many different leaders in a loosely organised resistance movement. The fact that Robin is traditionally based in the centuries preceding that of the Peasants' Revolt lends support to that view. However, the legend developed into romance, with characters added at the whim of later chroniclers.

It was only later that I read of witchcraft, of 'Rabbin' leaders of the mediaeval cult, and still later of the considerable esoteric theory about King Arthur and the Grail Romances. When Richard

Carpenter, who wrote the scripts for 'Robin of Sherwood', got Arthur involved in the story I was annoyed, thinking that he was just dragging in mythical figures to flesh out the rather sketchy legends. But then something began to dawn on me.

I thought back to my childhood. I had been a very sickly child, and my parents had been hard pressed to provide me with reading matter in those far off days before videos and daytime TV. It was then that I read of Robin, Arthur and the rest. This period had its beneficial effects; when I was seven years old my reading age was estimated at that of an average fourteen-year old. As I thought back to this period though, it was not those heroic tales that I remembered. It was the Readers' Digest!

During one of my sick periods I had somehow got hold of a pile of old copies of the Digest. Being very methodical, I arranged them in date order and began reading the earliest, from the late 1940s. In this there was a section that still appears occasionally, called 'Humour In Uniform'. Here serving men and ex-servicemen (and the very occasional woman) got a few dollars for telling amusing tales they had experienced. Most of these were still from World War II, but one, that somehow stuck in my memory, was from the period after the end of that war, when Germany was still divided into French, English, American and Russian zones. The writer claimed to have been stationed at a border post between, I think, the American and Russian zones. He claimed that every morning a man would ride a bicycle loaded with vegetables into the Russian zone. He and his basket of food would be searched, but nothing was ever found. In the evening he would return and be searched again, and again nothing was found. Finally, he turned up one day and announced that he was retiring, inviting the guards to a celebratory party at his house. When the guards arrived they discovered that he had a huge house, and was obviously very rich.

"Where did you get all this money?" They asked.
"From my smuggling, of course." He answered.
"But we searched you thoroughly, what were you you smuggling?"
"Bicycles."

I cannot say why this story stuck in my mind, but it did. As I grew older I developed a strong interest in religion, mythology and magic, and one day about twenty years later I settled down to read a book of Sufi teaching stories. These tales were told by the mystics of Islam as a popular way of transmitting their doctrines of mindfulness and awareness, and in this book, with a note that the tale was first collected in a book in the 11th century A.D., was a story about a man who used to ride a donkey laden with vegetables from Persia into Turkey each morning.......... and it was the same story.

I realised then that the similarities I had once noted between the tales of Robin and Arthur on the one hand, and the Indian epic known as the Ramayana were perhaps not co-incidental. Before that moment I had subscribed to the Jungian theory that significant tales would appear independently in different cultures. I was no longer happy with conventional views of historical development, that tended to look upon national, racial or religious boundaries as impenetrable barriers, across which no ideas ever crossed, but I suddenly realised that jokes and stories had a life of their own.

For a year or more I concentrated on the Arthur legends, and then turned to other matters. Gradually, however, Robin began to appear everywhere. It became obvious that there was no single source of the legend as we know it. Rather, he had become the focus towards which stories had gravitated, from Saxon resistance to the Normans to tales from ancient Egypt, from pre-Christian pagan beliefs to age-old Indian epics.

This book attempts to unravel the different strands of the Robin myth, as well as restoring some of the significance lost in the last century, when Anglo-Saxonism combined with Victorian prudishness to sever the connections between Robin, the Morris dance and the Mayday celebrations. It will achieve its purpose if it succeeds in establishing that Robin has become just as significant a figure in the mysteries of Britain as Arthur himself.

Finally, a rather important note. I will NOT be dealing with any of the supposed 'real' Robin Hood figures. There are many books outlining a Robert Hoode here, people with the surname Robinhood there, as well as the occasional real dispossessed nobleman living in the forests. Apart from the fact that the vast majority of these lived too late to be the Robin who served Good King Richard so faithfully, they would only, anyway, be 'hooks', upon which other material has been hung. The very fact that they, unlike Hereward the Wake or King Alfred, were unable to fix the stories in their own time indicates to me their irrelevance. It was not they who became the stuff of legend, merely the excuse for it. That early records show names similar to that of Robin Hood merely proves how popular a name it was, possibly becoming a nickname for anyone living outside the Norman law in the still extensive forests, and this book attempts to show why and how that happened.

CHAPTER ONE

THE ARCHERS IN THE FOREST

SOME time around 2000 BC a group of peoples began to spread out from a homeland somewhere in the Caucasus, although no-one is exactly sure about the point of origin, and the various archaeological theories are too complex to go into here. They went in every direction; to the north went the ancestors of the Russians, to the east went the first Indian Upper Castes, to the south went the Hittites and Persians and to the west the ancestors of most modern Europeans.

These people, known as the Indo-Europeans (the term Aryan having gone out of favour over the last fifty years for obvious reasons), took with them both a language and a culture. They valued the skills and bravery of the warrior, and the epic tales and poetry that they often inspired, but they were also skilful traders, artisans and artists. For more than a hundred years our view of them has been coloured by the fact that most of the epics are about war; after all, who would want to listen to 'The Saga Of Eric The Merchant, How He Travelled To The Land Of The West And Got A Really Good Deal Exchanging Turnips For Wool'. Although, having said that, it has been suggested that the tale of Jason And The Argonauts refers to early trading missions from Greece to Armenia. In Britain the first definite Indo-Europeans were amongst those peoples classified as Celts.

The Indo-Europeans should not be regarded as simply a race. By the beginning of written European history many peoples had been drawn into their cultural net, including black Iberian tribes of the Goidelic Celts who are now represented linguistically only in Ireland, Scotland and in the law-making rituals of the House of Keys in the Isle of Man, since Manx, like Cornish, has died as a spoken language. These Celts came northward along the Atlantic coast while the Brythonic Celts, ancestors of the Welsh, Cornish, and Breton peoples, as well as a lot of the English, moved westward from the European mainland, to be followed by the Saxons in post-Roman times. The Saxons, it should be noted, would probably have been classified as Celtic by the Greeks who first used the term Keltoi to describe the barbarians of the North, but by the time of the Saxon settlement the Romans had distinguished between Celts and Germans, a distinction that is more linguistic and religious than cultural, given that the essential interests of the Saxons and Celts were much the same.

However, the first Indo-Europeans to arrive in Britain found a highly sophisticated culture in place already. These were the Neolithic or 'Beaker' peoples, named for a particular style of drinking vessel. These were the builders of the astronomically-aligned stone circles, the long-barrows, dolmens and henges. They were probably related to todays Basque peoples, whose language resembles no other. There has been some talk of the Neoliths being 'proto-Celtic', but I feel that this confuses the issue, which becomes clearer when we consider the Indo-European attitude towards alien cultures.

Today it is easy, though usually accurate, to condemn Europeans for obliterating the cultures of those who come into contact with them, and this has led many of the more spiritual members of the modern world to seek for enlightenment elsewhere. There is great value to be derived from learning about, even immersing oneself in other spiritual traditions, but the modern white attitude towards other races was not always the case. Indeed, it was only with the advent of Christianity with its one-book, one-god, one-way attitude that the idea of superiority arose, along with the need for some moral defence of the appalling slave trade.

Historically the Indo-Europeans were highly receptive to the

6

culture of those they met. In India the Dravidians, and in Britain the Druids had considerable influence upon the incomers, so that by the time they began to write their beliefs down their religions differed enormously. The idea that Druidism was a Celtic invention can be discounted by the direction of its spread, which was in the opposite direction to that of the Celts themselves. Rather, it was a highly sophisticated mixture of Celtic and pre-Celtic religion developed in the British Isles, and one that seems to have developed along almost (but not quite) identical lines amongst both the Goidels and the Brythons. This movement spread into Gaul and led to the repression of Druidism by the Roman authorities, who had been wary of close ties between continental and British Celts since the time of Julius Caesar.

The same is true of the artistic nature of the British Celts, which differs radically from that of the now lost Celtic cultures elsewhere in Europe. Instead it shows a steady progressive development from that of the Neolithic men and women who carved such designs as the magnificent, intricate swirls on the huge stones at the entrance to the New Grange mound in Eire to the elaborate borders of the Book of Kells.

However, even the Neolithic culture was not the first in Britain. In the Mesolithic age peoples, probably related to the modern day Lapps and with a lifestyle still found both in Siberia and in the wilderness of Canada, had herded reindeer across the open areas and through the dense woodland at its edge. However, as the climate warmed up the ice retreated, and a great forest grew up that was unsuitable for reindeer, who have no immunity to many of the parasites found in temperate zones and would anyway be too warm, given their magnificently efficient fur. This led to the great Wildwood, the broad-leaf forests full of Elk, Bear, Boar, Wolf and the great Auroch, the extinct European Bison. These forests began growing about 8000 years ago.

Although conventional archaeologists would like there to be a clean break between the Mesolithic and Neolithic peoples, it is highly unlikely that all such peoples left with the reindeer. The evidence of folklore in the British Isles and the Continent constantly gives hints of a people of a type still found throughout the world today: forest people.

Forest peoples, whether in Malaya, Africa or South America, are classified as hunter-gatherers. They hunt for meat and generally only search for vegetables, although some show basic gardening skills with regards to certain staple foods, such as yams and cassava. There are, and have been, many types of hunter-gatherer societies, ranging from the Native Americans of the Great Plains to the Bushmen of the Kalahari Desert, but those found in forests show certain common tendencies. They tend to be small, they tend to blend in with their environment, but above all they tend to be archers (although they often know of local herbal poisons that have also led to the development of the blowpipe in various different forest cultures). They also tend to be small in number, living in extended families of between forty and a hundred. Their interests are diametrically opposed to those of the farmers who are usually to be found around the edge of the forests, and the Neolithic peoples of Britain were certainly agriculturalists.

The significance of the bow to the forest peoples is considerable. Both its direct use and the 'twang' it makes play a part in shamanic rituals. In South America some tribes believe that this sound acually attracts their prey. It is often the main musical instrument of the tribe, and of course it is the origin of the harp, so beloved of the Celts and, possibly, their Neolithic precursors.

It is important to realise the radical development that the Neolithic peoples represent. The fact that we are talking about a clash between 'Middle Stone Age' (Mesolithic) and 'New Stone Age' (Neolithic) peoples is distracting, the difference between the two is far greater than that between the Neolithic and Bronze Age peoples. Indeed, it is now believed that these were probably the same peoples, and certainly copper was used in Neolithic times, leading some historians to assign the word 'Chalcolithic' (copper-stone) instead. We know from the vitrified remains of a neolithic town at Catal Huyuk in Turkey, where volcanic eruptions froze several moments in time at different points over a three thousand year period beginning in 6000 B.C., that they wove cloth, using more than one weave, were skilful potters and in Britain we have the evidence of the Avebury complex, and in Ireland there is the New Grange complex, that shows a society that was highly organised, could undertake major building projects and therefore rather more numerous than any forest-dwelling tribe.

It was during the Neolithic period that the first forest clearances began, with meadows expanded into fields and low-lying valleys turned into farms. But this was only a minor affair compared with later developments. We also know that there is evidence of killing-grounds, small spaces cleared into which animals would be chased and shot down, but this practice goes back to the Mesolithic. It is probable that for a long time the two peoples lived side by side. Certainly the forest, the ancient Greenwood, was considered a source of both food and fuel well into the current century.

If we look at Congolese society we can get a glimpse of how relations between the Neoliths and the forest people might have been. The Congolese farmers of modern Zaire live peacefully but uneasily with the Pygmies. They meet, trade and talk occasionally, but they do not intermingle much, and hardly ever consider inter-marrying. Moreover, while the Pygmies of the rain forest are rather indifferent towards the farmers, the farmers hold a superstitious fear of the pygmies.

During the Simba uprising in the 1960s it was known that Congolese women who had married white men, fearful for the safety of their half-caste children, sometimes hid them with the friendly pygmies, knowing that the Simba guerrillas were too scared of the forest people to dare attack them. Similar attitudes can be found in South America, where the social similarities with the Pygmies is striking, so much so that to speculate on British Mesolithic ways from modern forest hunter-gatherers is perfectly acceptable. The forest has its own rules, and those who live there have to fit in with them. It is also noticeable that both African and South American tribes place a great value upon honey, often regarded as the most precious and special of commodities. The first national alcoholic drink recorded in Britain was, of course, mead.

If there was, as I suspect, a forest-dwelling community living alongside the pre-Celtic farmers of Britain, we would have little physical trace of them today. Forest dwellers do not always have permanent villages, but tend to move around the forest, often once a year, when it is easier to do so than to search further and further away for their food. It is quite common to ceremonially burn their houses, since new ones can be quickly constructed when they choose their new site. Within a few years no trace is left, the forest has reclaimed the village and the vegetation that they have stripped has returned.

This highly ecological method of living enables certain tribes in New Guinea, who are part-way between the hunter-gatherer and agricultural stage, to circle around a mountain about once every fifty years without ever permanently damaging their habitat. They even have certain taboos against cutting away particular weeds from their gardens, and these are the ones that will enable gardens to revert to raw forest quickly, allowing both plant and animal stocks to return. Obviously, if no trace of a Mesolithic peoples can be found after half a century, none can be expected after thousands of years. Only hard, durable artefacts wait to be dug up.

Their arrowheads, being flint, cannot be carbon dated, so whenever an arrowhead is found it is 'dated' by archaeologists to the Mesolithic period. This is only justifiable if we think of the Neolithic peoples as having wiped out the Mesoliths at once. Given the low rate of forest clearance during the Neolithic and Bronze Age periods, they would surely have remained hidden in the forests, just as their South American equivalents do today. The Mesolithic peoples would have known the forests extremely well. Hunting them would be difficult, assuming such a genocidal policy was ever practiced, since they would just seem to vanish into the Greenwood. Just like the Fairy Folk of Celtic lore.

What evidence do we have of this? Two types. The first is folklore. It was virtually accepted fact in the last century that such peoples survived in Scottish and other legends. The Fairy Archers were much feared in the Glen where, according to the old poem;

"We dare not go a-hunting
For fear of little men."

When flint arrowheads were found they were known as Fairy Arrows, and Welsh legend occasionally tells of people being found dead in the forest, with lots of tiny arrows the cause. The advent of modern Archaeology, with its great love of scientific equipment and fancy definitions, has forced this theory to the fringes of prehistoric research, but I do not think that this is justified. Indeed, writers in the last century commonly spoke of 'primitive pygmies' dwelling in ancient Britain, and these authors were no doubt inspired by comparing folklore with the discoveries involved in the 'opening up' of Africa then underway.

The second type of evidence is archaeological. There are the arrowheads, the killing-grounds of course, but recently a stunning discovery in the Alps has added a new dimension.

In 1991 the perfectly preserved body of a Bronze Age man was found embedded in ice on the Austrian-Italian border. He was apparently involved in 'mining', digging for nuggets of copper or ore. In this early stage of the hunt for metals a great deal of ore-bearing rock lay close to, or indeed on the surface, so although to talk of him being a 'miner' is accurate, it does not necessarily mean that his people sank great shafts deep into the side of mountains, although they certainly did begin to hollow out existing caves. However, he was also carrying a bow, not surprising for someone searching in the mountains, who might have chanced upon dinner 'on the hoof' as he crossed the icy range, but it was soon realised that some of the arrows he was carrying were unfinished, so of no real use. Early reports suggested that the bow and the 14 arrows he carried had some religious significance.

Why would a bow and arrows be seen as powerful? As a talisman, it would surely be connected with the men of the forest. Just as the present-day Congolese regard the pygmies with awe and dread, so the Neoliths must have feared the silent archers of the forest, and legends of 'little people' associated with mines, particularly in the Scandinavian and Cornish regions, makes one wonder whether some Mesoliths used these as hide-outs from the newcomers, or even searched them for the material for makeshift jewellery, as still happens in the Amazon. As yet the Celts, with their knowledge of Iron, had yet to arrive. When they did, great swathes of forest would be cleared to provide charcoal for the smelting of Iron in the blast furnaces, that had to be far hotter than the ordinary furnaces needed to smelt Copper and Tin to make Bronze. When that happened, the forest peoples would no doubt fight back, but eventually would retreat to the most out the way places, eventually to disappear or even merge with Neolithic populations. In the last century there was considerable research into certain features found in localised communities in Britain that did not fit the normal Indo-European or specifically Celtic type, such as the black curly hair of South Wales and the phenomenon of 'gingerness'. This suggests that pockets of Celtic peoples retained pre-Celtic racial characteristics, and evidence of small, closely knit communities bearing common, unusual features are even known from pre-war Lancashire.

The archers in the forest would live, however, in myth and folk tale. The Celts, whose arrival would have created the greatest clashes with these peoples, would remember them, as would the Saxons, whose experiences in and around the great forests of Germany would have been similar. They would have told tales of bands of men and women who could strike without warning, whose marksmanship was extraordinary, whose camps moved constantly, making it impossible to find them. Eventually these tales would be added to the lore of Robin Hood.

CHAPTER TWO

THE DIVINE BOWMAN

THE Indo-European people have always loved the epic. In written form we have many of these, from the Trojan Wars to the tales of Charlemagne. These sagas all tell tales of heroism, interspersed with humour, whimsy and bawdy. They were originally memorised by professionals, the Fili and Bards of Ireland being one example, but were committed to writing when the advantages of that medium became obvious. Nevertheless, in present day Turkey there are still story-tellers who can repeat, word for word, a tale lasting up to nine hours, just as African specialists can repeat the history of a village going back several hundred years.

In India, where the effects of Christianity have been least felt amongst the Indo-Europeans, these sagas have become scriptures. They rate below the Vedas, the oldest living scriptures in the world, and the Upanishads, the post-Buddhist philosophical commentaries on the Vedas, but these sagas are the basis of the Vaishnava Bhakti faiths. The Bhakti faiths are the most popular of the Hindu religions, and the Vaishnava Bhakti sects consist of personal devotion to one particular human incarnation, or Avatar, of the God Vishnu. The Shaivite Bhaktis worship Shiva, a pre-Indo-European deity who has, as used to be the way, fitted in quite comfortably with the religion of the conquerors.

There are two great Indian epics. The most popular is the Mahabharata, which is four times as long as the Bible. This tells of Krishna, an incarnation of the God Vishnu who acts both as

13

charioteer and spiritual adviser to Prince Arjuna, one of the pro-
tagonists in the Mahabharata, a name which has the same linguistic
root and meaning as 'Major Battle'. This, like the Ramayana, is
believed to have been first written down at around the time of
Christ, or up to two centuries later, but as an oral tradition they are
considerably older. When they truly date from is difficult to say, but
two things are certain. The events in the Mahabharata date back to real
events that took place before written Indian history, rather like the
events in the Iliad, which relate back to prehistoric Greece. And
secondly, there can be no doubt that the events remembered in the
Ramayana are even earlier.

It is central to Vaishnava faith that Krishna was the latest
human incarnation of Vishnu, who shall nevertheless appear at the
end of the current era as Kalki, the white horse. It is specifically
stated that Rama lived earlier, that he was the previous incarnation
of Vishnu. Since the Ramayana has the status of holy scripture, the
tale, which is highly popular with Indian children, is overladen with
religious material. It is, incidentally, supposed to have been written
by a robber who 'disappeared' after a visit from the Gods to learn
how to tell the tale, a theme that later appears in Ireland! However,
it is easy enough to draw out the basic story behind the religious
overlay of several millenia. When we do so we can see, clearly, that
this ancient Indian tale must date back to the earliest periods of
Indo-European story-telling. The Ramayana clearly contains the
same mythical elements, and many of the same events, as both the
Arthurian romances and the Robin Hood stories.

It might be possible, one day, to reconstruct the original tale,
if there was a single source. On the other hand, it may be that Rama
inherited two separate tales that stayed distinct in the Celtic and
Saxon worlds. One way or the other, to demonstrate the link I will
retell, very swiftly, the tale of Rama, pointing out the similarities.

Rama was born eldest son of the King of the Solar Dynasty of
Ayodhya, the Maharajah Dasaratha, but he was not merely a Prince.
He was in fact the incarnation of Vishnu, the preserver, of the Hindu
Triad of Gods. (This triad seems to be of Dravidian origin, since the

names of two of the deities are not found elsewhere in the Indo-European traditions and Vishnu was only a minor deity in the Vedas. Shiva is certainly Rudra, the antler-headed deity who was worshipped in Harappa and Mohenjo-Dara before the Indo-Europeans arrived). In his youth he was taken away from the palace and instructed by the mystic Vishwamitra. He demonstrated his divinity by lifting, stringing, drawing and breaking a bow dropped by the god Shiva during a heavenly battle, which no other man had even been able to lift, and in doing so won the hand of Sita, princess of the Lunar Dynasty of Mithila where the bow had fallen.

Arthur was truly the son of Uther Pendragon, but was adopted by Ector, who sent him away to be instructed by the mystic Merlin. He demonstrated his heirship by raising a sword embedded in a stone by magical means that no other had been able to remove. He soon marries Guinevere, and in the western esoteric tradition these are seen as archetypical Solar and Lunar figures. Robin wins Marian by an archery contest, but only after she has been kidnapped (see below). Both Rama and Robin are always depicted with bow and quiver.

Rama soon becomes master of the Bow, acquiring another one dropped by Indra, the Indo-European God whose name is related to 'Andrew' (Manly). He is due to inherit the Kingdom, but by trickery the throne goes to his half-brother. As a result he retreats to the forests to avoid being the focus of any dissent. Here there are many sages who meditate and sacrifice to the Gods. However, many demons, ruled by the demon King of Ceylon, interrupt them by flying overhead and defile their sacrifices by flinging corpses onto their altars. Rama, his brother Lakshmana and his wife Sita see this, and Rama and his brother begin a war against these demons, shooting them down with arrows. This enrages the Demon King, Ravana, who sends a force to kidnap Sita and take her to his palace, where his efforts at seduction are fruitless. Rama gains the aid of Hanuman, the Monkey God, who marshals millions of monkeys to attack Ceylon, where they rescue Sita and return to the forest.

Robin is due to inherit Huntingdon (in the most popular versions) but is tricked out of it. He retires to the forest with a group of men. The locals are harassed by representatives of the Evil King John, who plague them with taxes. Robin fights them off, so to capture him the Sheriff of Nottingham kidnaps Marian, Robin's true love, and announces an archery contest. Robin's men enter the castle, and when he wins the contest a fight ensues, after which he rescues Marian and returns to the forest.

Rama is eventually given the kingdom, which he rules wisely, creating a Golden Age that Indians still look back to as the ideal Indian kingdom, indeed Mahatma Gandhi died with the name of Rama on his lips. However, court gossip insists that Sita must have had sex with the Demon King, even if under duress, and although she proves her purity the gossip continues and she is forced back to the forest, where she gives birth to Rama's twin sons, having concealed her pregnancy. He is forced, through duty, to remain King. One day he leads a hunting expedition into the forest, where his sons, thinking someone has come to attack their mother, kill him.

Arthur's court is wracked by gossip about Guinevere, who really has betrayed him with a noble from across the water in the form of Lancelot. He is forced to send her away. Eventually he is mortally wounded by his illegitimate son fathered upon Morgan-Le-Fay who is half-Fairy, and adopts the form of Guinevere to seduce Arthur. In the Ramayana a Demon woman adopts the form of Sita to seduce Rama, but fails.

Both Arthur and Rama are expected to return. Arthur is spirited away to the Isle of Avalon to await the day when Britain needs him again. Vishnu arises from the body of Rama, and does indeed return as Krishna.

The similarities are obvious, but so are the differences. Arthur, being the subject of Christian thinking, is a flawed hero, and his wife is portrayed in the spiteful way common to the Christian exoteric attitude towards women. Rama, being a god, is flawed only in that his marriage is deliberately delayed by the Goddess Maya to avoid the astrologically perfect moment, otherwise the events in the Ramayana would not take place and the demons would never be defeated. His wife is also divine, indeed, it was she who first lifted the bow of Shiva when, as a little girl, she retrieved a ball that had rolled under it, much to the astonishment of the royal court.

The monkeys of the story may well be memories of the same mesolithic peoples that inspired part of the Robin legend, especially that which comes from the forest-dwelling sprite known as Robin Goodfellow or Jack-in-the-green. The fact that Robin is not himself a King, merely a dispossessed nobleman, will be dealt with in the next chapter.

Rama is by no means the only divine bowman. There is Cupid/ Eros with his arrows of love, and on the downside one is reminded of Nimrod, that mighty 'hunter before the Lord', who built the tower of Babel in order to fire an arrow into heaven. There is, however, no clear link between Eros and Robin, and there are many divine beings in many traditions with as many different weapons. In the Ramayana the significance is not just the concept of the divine bowman, it is the story, the character, indeed the identity of Rama with both Robin and Arthur that is clear.

The Ramayana is not the origin of the Arthurian and Robin Hood legends, they merely have the same source or sources. However, tales do travel, Buddha having become a Saint (Jehosaphat) in such a way, and it would be impossible to say precisely when and how they influenced each other. My suspicion is that both have their roots in an ancient Indo-European saga, and that whereas Rama inherited all of the original elements, those that didn't fit some historical event from the Celto-Saxon wars were left to be picked up by Robin, who as we shall see inherited a considerable number of other elements as well.

CHAPTER THREE

GOOD KING, BAD KING

WE have already seen that Rama and Arthur represent the ideal King, but Robin himself is merely a noble, and in the original tales was merely a stout Saxon yeoman from the village of Locksley. It is precisely this discrepancy that led me to concentrate on the Arthurian connection for so long, at the expense of Robin. The connection between ideal Kingship, a constant concern of Indo-European lore, and the Robin stories only begins to make sense when we examine the central theme of the whole myth, that of the struggle between King Richard the Lionheart and his brother John. This not only explains the connection, it explains why the Robin stories became fixed in that era, and also why modern films constantly show a certain historical anomaly that I shall deal with later.

There is a theme that runs throughout tales of Kingship, that of the evil brother. The extent of this evil varies, Romulus and Remus merely quarrel over what name their proposed city is to take, although with fatal consequences. Interestingly enough, it is Romulus who is the evil one and who kills the younger twin Remus, although this version of the legend was told by republican Romans to explain their abolition of Kingship. The early senators become so tired of the tyranny of Romulus that they cut his body into pieces and hide them beneath their togas.

The most famous example of this tale is again found in a non-Christian religion, that of Egypt. The religion of Egypt was not fixed throughout its history, and neither was its mythology. At different times Egypt was two separate kingdoms, then later was united. Different peoples gained the upper hand, and consequently we have variations of a considerable nature in the tales.

The theme of ideal, divinely ordained kingship is at its strongest in Egypt, and may have directly influenced the Japanese to invent the myth of the Divine Emperor. Indeed Osiris is seen as a God, whereas Romulus becomes a God merely to placate his father, Mars. His son Horus, the Egyptian Mars, is also a God, as well as being the first Pharaoh. However, central to the Egyptian theme is that of the Bad, usurping King.

The Bad King is needed to demonstrate what happens if the wrong person gains power. As such, the bad example is as important as the ideal ruler in the stories of such monarchs. Of all such tales, that of Osiris and Set is probably the most influential. If it seems unlikely that ancient Egyptian tales could have influenced Robin Hood stories, remember that Isis and Osiris were worshipped well into the fourth century AD, and thus the myth that was central to their cult was known throughout the Roman Empire, including in Britain where there was a thriving temple in London, some nine centuries before the Robin tales were supposed to have happened. That's about the same time-span separating the Turkish donkey smuggler and the German bicycle smuggler, and while there were Isians in London, I don't think that there were that many Sufis in the U.S.Army! Anyway, it is the tenor of the tale that is important here.

There are two versions of the story of Osiris and Set, sometimes combined into one. In both, Osiris is ruler of Egypt, but his evil brother Set kills him and hides the body. Isis, wife and sister of Osiris, discovers the body and is able to resurrect him for one night. She subsequently gives birth to Horus, who grows to manhood and overthrows his Uncle to become the first Pharaoh.

In one version of the story, the most famous, the body of Osiris is cut into twelve pieces and hidden in various places in Egypt, just

20

as the body of Romulus is cut into pieces and hidden in the senators' togas. In the other he is hidden in a tree from which he emerges when Isis discovers him. This latter version somehow became a myth in Druidism, where during the Roman occupation Osiris (Ausar in Egyptian) becomes Esus. The emergence of a divine King from the tree, especially the Oak, is repeated in England where the Druidic cult of the Oak is continued in the many Royal Oaks, Honor Oaks, Robin Hood's Oaks and of course the many oaks associated with the future Charles II.

The key elements of this story are of the wrong, bad king usurping his good, just brother, and the good king's miraculous return for one last appearance. The psychology of this rebirth is associated with the peculiar nature of Egypt, essentially a long thin riverside farm. The death of Osiris was associated with winter and the rebirth with the first shoots of the new, green corn in spring. The headdress of Osiris resembles such a shoot making him the first known Green Man figure, as well as being vaguely phallic. The story of Osiris, Set and Horus was enacted publicly once a year as part of the annual cycle of Egyptian festivals that mirrored the growing cycle of the all-important corn. This included a ritual battle, which as we shall see is an essential part of the cycle.

It was the corn of Egypt that made it a target for so many conquerors, including the Romans, who took the cult of Isis and Serapis, a specifically fertility-based version of Osiris, all over the empire, including to Britain. Egypt was known as the bread-basket of the Roman Empire, but as the empire expanded another source was needed. This was, surprisingly enough, Britain, where Celtic agriculture attained a level of yield-per-acre not reached again until the nineteenth century. This is why many army-inspired rebellions started in Britain, including that of the future Emperor Constantine. As such it is hardly surprising that Serapis, who wears the corn-measure upon his head, was a popular Romano-British deity.

Versions of the theme, such as Romulus and Remus, are found in various cultures, but in the Robin Hood stories it is clear that it is Richard and John who play the roles. This book was first presented, in a shorter form, at a conference held in Charlton House in South London, and it was while researching the history of the house that I gained the important clue that explained the role of John in the tales.

Charlton was the site of a pagan survival called the Horn Fair. Until a riotous brawl between Bermondsey dockers and Woolwich army cadets led to its being banned in the middle of the 19th century, every year on October 18th people would process from Cuckolds' Point in Bermondsey to Charlton Village. The men would be dressed as women, a theme found elsewhere in this book, and all would wear horns, blow horns, carry horns upon poles and at the fair would buy trinkets carved from horn. When they first arrived they would walk around the church of St.Luke, whose feast day is October the 18th, three times, before getting down to the serious business of having fun. According to the saying of the time "All is fair at Charlton Fair", including the practice of hitting swaggering members of the more prosperous classes on their jutting elbows with gigantic ladles.

In my researches I discovered two quite separate legends concerning the origin of this obviously pagan observance. In the first it was stated, as early as the beginning of the 1600s, that there had once been a temple to 'Dame Fortune', i.e. the Roman Goddess Fortuna, at Bermondsey, and that when the temple was destroyed the effects were moved to Charlton, where this was subsequently remembered in the annual fair. This has the ring of truth about it. Fortuna carried the Cornucopia horn of plenty, which is shown at Charlton House. Built in 1617, it has an arch topped by two of them. Fortuna would have been linked with Cerridwen by the Romano-British Celts, whose cauldron could feed an army. It may well be that Cuckolds' Point is a corruption of Cornucopia.

There is, however, another tale. This states that one fine day King John was riding through the fields of Bermondsey when he chanced upon the local mill. The miller himself was not at home, but his wife was, and when the miller returned home he discovered John busy cuckolding him. Before he could vent his wrath, John revealed his identity and offered, by way of restitution, all the land that the miller could see from his front door. The miller, being at the foot of the Blackheath plateau, consequently gained all the land from Bermondsey to Charlton. The horns are thus the 'cuckolds horns' believed to grow on the head of a wronged husband. A variant of this story has the miller given all the land within earshot of a mighty blast upon a hunting horn.

Historically this makes no sense at all. Not only was John unlikely to give away millions of pounds worth of land to a cuckolded peasant, his sarcastic nickname, Lackland, reminds us that he had no land to offer, all of it being inherited by Richard according to the strict 'primogeniture' rule of the feudal system. What is more, this legend is found in various parts of England. It is, of course, a 'just-so' story, as Rudyard Kipling named them, to explain away rather than to truly explain. But if the real event could not have taken place, and the Horn Fair was a thousand years old, why did John get lumbered with the story?

The reality of life under Richard and John is rather different from that as told in the Robin Hood legends. Richard was an appalling King. He spent about three months in England, far preferring his French possessions, and his main interest in England was as a source of taxes. These paid for his genocidal crusading adventures, depicted with refreshing realism in the film 'Robin and Marian', of which more later. John, however, was rather better. He concentrated upon England, and used tax money to improve the country, eventually becoming so unpopular with the feudal barons that, beneath a sacred oak at Runnymead, he created the first parliament to satisfy them. Meanwhile Richard fell out with another murderous European ruler who imprisoned him and demanded ransom. This was never paid, and according to legend his personal minstrel, Blondel, travelled Europe searching for him. This is hardly likely given the fact that his whereabouts were no great secret, but this quest from one castle to another is remarkably similar to the myth of Isis searching for the body, or the bits of the body, of Osiris.

Richard and John, then, took on mythical roles, to which the practical realities of running a country were irrelevant. John, who had had to organise the over-taxing of England on his brother's behalf, became the same, bad usurping king that Set had been, while the absentee landlord became the hero, wandering around not too far from Egypt, representing the ideal king. Thus John became the cuckolder in some old tales, and the enemy of Robin Hood in others.

In the Robin Hood myth, Robin becomes the substitute for Richard. He too is dispossessed, but unlike Richard he is able to wage war upon the usurping ruler and his local representative, the Sheriff of Nottingham. His own loss of land is linked to John, and he states openly that he is a loyal subject of Richard. In the modern films this is made absolutely clear, and whether Robin is Errol Flynn (himself a figure much associated with fertility) or even a cartoon fox, there is a scene at the end when Richard himself emerges, like Osiris or Esus, from the green trees to ratify Robin's battle. It goes without saying that nothing remotely like this could have happened, but it must be seen to happen. Like Horus, Robin must win the day, which he usually does in those many films whose makers feel unable to kill him off for fear of disappointing audiences or ruining the possibility of sequels. Once again, John becomes the explanation for another pagan observance, but this is dealt with in Chapter Five.

The historical facts around King John, that he actually won, ruin the chances for Robin to fulfil the Horus role, and Richard never fulfilled the role of Agnar, of whom more in the next chapter. With Robin as with Arthur it is the treachery of a woman that destroys him. But he inherits a role as old as that of Rama, defender of the Good King against his evil brother, and so another layer is added to his tales.

CHAPTER FOUR

ROBIN AND ODIN

THE name of Robin Hood has always been problematic. The earliest explanation of the legend is that it was one Robert, not Robin, who was dispossessed of his estate at Huntingdon. Andrew Collins has discovered that the King of Scotland used to inherit this land, but that the title to it was held in abeyance while Robert the Bruce was winning the throne, suggesting an origin for that part of the tale.

In spite of the legends that Robin may have been Norman, or even Scottish, the most common assumption by researchers is that he was of Saxon stock, though from an area once colonised by Vikings and thus possibly of mixed Germanic background. This is borne out in a way by his name. Remembering that we are not dealing with any one historical person, the name Hood points to a connection with Saxon paganism, as does Robin, although the actual word may well be Celtic.

The Saxons who settled in Britain are often portrayed as bloodthirsty invaders who only became 'properly' British when they accepted Christianity. The truth is rather different. For a start, they did not invade Britain as such. Pagan Saxons had been arriving on the East Coast for more than a century before their increasing numbers began to alarm the largely Christianised Romano-British Celts. Their right to do so was as a result of properly ratified, if unwise, treaties. What is more, they did not, as is often stated, drive all of the Celts into Wales and Cornwall.

Our first 'English' literature, such as the Anglo-Saxon chronicle, is not written in a truly Saxon language. Anglo-Saxon is rather a patois, with so many Celtic words in it that only its grammar makes it a Germanic language, rather than the unique and separate Indo-European language it was to develop into. The Saxons merged with the peasants of the Celtic population, who in Kent at least had only moved from Belgium at around the time of the Roman invasions, with only the leadership passing from Celts to the Germans. The result of this merger, later Danish influence and the development of Anglo-Norman, was the first West European language to abandon gender in grammar, our English tongue.

As languages merged, so did people. Like most Indo-Europeans, the Celts and Saxons found no difficulty with this and a new, combined culture began to develop, but both the Saxons and the later Vikings brought with them a vigorous new element, Odinism and the associated Runelore.

Odinism was not a truly ancient cult. Odin, identified as Woden or Wotan, after whom Wednesday is named, was originally not the chief object of Germanic worship. The Germanic peoples, like most Indo-Europeans, originally worshipped a storm God, Thor, who equates with Jupiter, Zeus, Indra and company. Semitic peoples also worshipped their storm God Baal, indicating a cross-cultural pattern of belief.

Odinism did not supplant the earlier Germanic paganism in anything like the Christian break from Judaism or the Buddhist break from early Brahmanism. Both the Saxons and the Vikings kept their old myths, merely shifting emphasis. One of these myths was that of Agnar and Geirrod, the sons of the King of the Goths, Hrauding. Like Romulus and Remus they were orphaned, or at least separated from their native land, during which time their father died. Geirrod, like John and Set the younger of the two royal brothers, attempted to kill Agnar, in this case by pushing him out to sea in a boat. He then returned to become King of the Goths, but was a terrible ruler, again like the archetypical Bad Kings of other mythologies. Agnar meanwhile drifted ashore in the land of Giants, where he married a Giantess. Odin decided to change this by adopting the guise of Grimnir, which significantly means 'the hooded one'. He confronts Geirrod, who falls upon his sword, and Agnar is restored to the throne.

Odin, however, is a both a warrior and a wisdom God, as well as being the God of poetry, the means by which all hero-tales were transmitted originally, either in India, Iceland or Ireland. The Celtic Druids, and the version of Christianity they developed before conversion to the Roman faith, already equated Jesus with Esus, and to this day it is common to speak in Hymns and Poems of Jesus hanging upon a tree, the Calvary Cross, in spite of the fact that a cross will not have been part of any living tree for some time. Odinism fitted in naturally, and the language of Odinism was adopted by the Church.

Odin had gained knowledge of the Runes by hanging from the world-Ash Yggdrasil for nine days to snatch them from the Norns, the three Goddesses of fate. As such, he was associated with trees, and although he cannot be seen as a tree-deity or a fertility god in pure Odinism, in England he soon became firmly linked with such concepts.

Odin discovered writing in the Saxon story, and in the Celtic world every letter is named for a tree. The original Druidic alphabet, Ogham, sounds close enough to Odin for erroneous connections to have been made. Odin's wild hunt was moved from the heavens to the forests that still covered much of England. He was seen as an old man, a shaman rather than a warrior, and his name passed into the pagan religion of England in many ways. Nevertheless, his association with the wild hunt, one that regarded no territorial laws, became important after the Normans invaded.

When Christianity came, it came bearing gifts. The early preachers of the Roman faith were only really concerned with converting Kings, offering the protection of the Emperor, whoever that was at the time, and unity with a wide religious empire. What's more, they were forced to accept the services of the Celtic Christian priesthood, who themselves were the heirs of pagan Druidism. These priests were married, and thus unable to become 'proper'

Romanish priests, but as the Culdees they carried out important priestly functions until the newer church was able to supply sufficient clerics. Even then, Culdee families carried on administering the mixed Christian-Pagan tradition. The peoples themselves were converted reluctantly, and they never truly adopted the new faith.

The Saxon pagan observances were gleefully accepted. To this day there is a tradition of decorating gables with simple patterns, and this is descended from the Saxon habit of placing protective runes over doors.In many parts of Britain pagan dances were carried out, which merged, as we shall see in the next chapter, with Morris dancing. However, such dances as the Abbots Bromley Horn Dance and the Helston Furry dance are far older, and slightly less exuberant practises are still carried out in parts of Germany. Once, every village in England would have had its ritual dances. Many of these involved a 'horse', a man dressed in horse costume who would 'cover' women with his skirts. This remnant of Celtic-Saxon horse worship was known in different parts of the country as the Hobby or Hooden horse. The dances were often led by a man dressed as a woman.

Hooden and Odin are too close to be co-incidental, so the Hooden Horse is surely Sleipnir, the horse of Odin. Odin easily becomes Hobby as well, and indeed Hob, meaning imp (short for impious=pagan) is very common, as in Hobgoblin.

I would suggest that both Robin and Hood are thus descended from the name of Odin. This duplication is very common in religion, from the Marmar (Mars twice) of the ancient Roman Arval brethren, to the JahJah (Jah = Jehovah twice) of modern Rastafarianism. Perhaps the Hood relates him directly to Odin, Robin to his nature as a spirit of the trees. The fact that he is nowadays shown as hooded, rather than capped, is a modern interpretation of the word Hood, as is T.H.White's suggestion that it is a corruption of Wood (White incidentally pushes back Robin to Arthurian times in his Arthurian series, the first volume of which Disney turned into a cartoon, The Sword In The Stone). There is,

28

however, a logic to each. Robin does indeed, through Odin, Esus and the Mesolithic connection, relate to the woods. He is also Hooded, even if he wears a cap, as shall be shown in the next chapter.

The Odinic phase of English paganism was brief, but strong and vigorous. There is considerable evidence that a great deal of the 'cunning' crafts, such as Witchcraft originally was, descend from Odinism and Saxon paganism. Mediaeval tales of a 'Rabbin' leading the covens suggests another link with the Robin/Odin figure, although, *pace* Margaret Murray, this may have been an inquisitors invention from Rabbi, and the rumour that witches danced with 'Robin Goodfellow', often depicted as the Pan/Satan figure beloved of the woodcuts of the middle ages is another pointer. I will say more of Robin Goodfellow later. Often these revels were supposed to take place in the woods, although heaths (hence 'heathen') were another favoured spot. The persistence of Odinic names in English country pagan survivals points to a merger between Celtic and Saxon practises that could have led to as interesting a religion as the merged language that, along with Anglo-Norman French, was to become our modern tongue. Christianity may have put paid to that, but it couldn't stop the development of the Robin Hood myth, to carry forward yet another layer of meaning, equating Robin Hood with Odin, the Hooded Grimnir, avenging the wrongfully disinherited king, right into the present day.

CHAPTER FIVE

A COUPLE OF LIKELY LADS

While it is clear that Anglo-Saxon culture was a mixture of Saxon and Celtic elements, and we have also seen that the primaeval tales that were to become those of Arthur and Robin reached India in the Ramayana, it would be difficult to support the connection if there were no uniquely Celtic elements that contributed to the stories. And though the Goidels and Brythons arrived in the British Isles from different directions, they are still more closely related to each other than either are to the Saxons and Danes, let alone the Indians. While there is a wealth of mainly Brythonic Celtic lore in the Arthurian cycle, it would be surprising if Robin did not inherit some of this material too, and indeed he does.

While it is obvious that Odin contributed something to both the legend and the name of Robin Hood, there is another character, indeed a God (though with one human parent) whose name is highly reminiscent of that of Robin. This is Gwynn Ap Nudd, whom Christianity was to relegate to being a mere chieftain of the faery race, in other words a lord of the 'hobs'. Since Gwynn is from the Brythonic cycle of myths, and must have been known in the areas that were later Saxonised, it would be surprising if the Hob Gwynn Ap Nudd contributed nothing to the legend of Robin Hood, especially since 'Hwd' means something akin to Magical in Welsh.

Robin Hood: The Spirit of the Forest

It is unfortunate that we have so little of Brythonic legend. We do have four sources: The Mabinogion, The Red Book of Hergest, the so-called Welsh Triads and the Black Book of Carmathen, but when we look at the enormous volume of Irish and Scottish material it is obvious that a great deal has been lost. Given the great Celtic love of story-telling in poetic form, it is obvious that the suppression of the Welsh Bards, more than half a millenium before the dispersal of the Irish Bards, is responsible for the scant material available. However, the Red Book of Hergest gives the outline of the myth of Gwynn Ap Nudd and we can see a connection that helps explain the linking of Robin with Mayday, which is dealt with in detail in a chapter of its own.

Gwynn Ap Nudd was Lord of the Underworld. As such he fulfils a role found in most Indo-European religion, where the king of the dead is to be feared but is not evil as such. A constant theme is that this figure yearns for the daylight world, and in the Welsh legend this takes the form of Gwynn's lust for the beautiful Creurdilad, which leads him to steal forth from his dark realm to capture her. In this he is like Robin, stealing forth from the dark of the Greenwood to capture Marian from the Sheriff. However, Gwynn has a rival, the solar figure of Gwyrthur Ap Greidayl, and this results in a glorious Celtic hero-battle for her hand. With Greidawl I am highly tempted to see an origin for the name of Guy of Gisborne, but perhaps that is stretching it a bit, although we shall see later that Guy is a well established character in the older tales. Perhaps he is also Geirrod, who Odin trounced on behalf of Agnar.

The battle for Creurdilad goes on and on until eventually King Arthur is called in to settle the matter. He decrees that the two shall fight for this fair maiden every May 1st, just as Robin fought for Marian on the same day in the Mayday celebrations of Mediaeval England and Scotland. This is thus surely the same story or, to be more precise, the element of the Gwynn myth that became attached to that of the Nordic Odin to create the essential framework of the Robin Hood story, albeit one that has diminished with the decline of traditional festivals.

32

The annual Mayday battle reflects the common mythic theme of the battle between the sterile winter period, represented by the underworld, and the power of fertility reborn in the spring. This is found in the Greek myth of the rape of Persephone, who must spend six months in Hades and six months in the daylight world, and in the Egyptian myth of Osiris and Set, who did annual battle in the seasonal myths of the fertility of the Nile. In the Mayday battle Robin has become the power of light and fertility, but this reversal is understandable. A similar switch is found between the myths of the ancient Indian and Persian scriptures, where the Indians have 'good' Deva Gods and bad 'Asura' Demons, while the Persians have bad Devas and good 'Ahuras'. With Robin identified with Odin and the power of the forest, now seen as a refuge from Norman tyranny rather than a place of terror, he takes the redemptive role while Guy/Gwyrthur becomes the villain of the piece.

The forest was also the place of the hunt, the main source of fresh food during the winter months, so Robin becomes associated with the Wild Hunt of Odin and Gwynn of the Winter. Indeed, those scholars with a Celtic bias associate the mediaeval myth of the Wild Hunt with Gwynn rather than Odin. This argument reflects a long battle between Celtic and Germanic historians that began in the 19th Century over the origin of British national myths. It is far more sensible, surely, to recognise the common origin and accommodating nature of the Indo-European Pagans and to realise that a merger of myth was inevitable.

The mythology of the Gaelic world is another matter. The Irish literary tradition, or at least that which still survives in its original form, began far earlier than any other in the British Isles and remained independent until the 17th century. By this time the Irish Gaels had colonised Scotland and their tradition went with them. As such, the Irish mythological tradition might be expected to inherit the same elements as those found in England and Wales, but without the same social context. These elements are found, and very strongly so, in the tales of Finn MacCumhail.

Gwynn means White, as does Finn, and both are the son of the

God of the Sky. They are both great hunters, and Celtic scholars agree that they have a common origin. But Finn is a far more developed character, and is clearly the inheritor of the whole basic collection of myths that we find in Arthur, Robin and Rama. Although supposedly based upon a real character of around 300 A.D. there can be no doubt that here we have yet another example of the Indo-European hero-king.

Finn is the hereditary leader of the Fenians, a group of semi-independent warriors devoted to the high king of Ireland. However, he is deprived of his right to lead when, as a boy, his father is killed by a rival clan. For his safety he is hidden with Druids, but in the Irish version of this common theme the Druids are women. He is, in other words, playing the same role as both Arthur and Rama, hiding in the forest and preparing to become the rightful leader.

When he wins his rightful place, a golden Fenian age begins. He defends the coasts against marauders much as Arthur did against the Saxons, but his band of men, greater than the Round Table Knights in number, live far more like Robin. Just as Robin and his men spend some time in the forest but others amongst the population, dining at the Blue Boar Inn for example, so Finn and his men spend the six months of winter with the people but the six of summer living off the land in the forests, hunting and training. This training, and the tests that would-be Fenians had to undergo, remind one of the Samurai as much as the Grail knights, and was surely beyond the real capabilities of any real mortal. They would have to stand waist-high in a pit and defend themselves from the blows of nine other men, for example. But the interesting aspects are those of being able to move through the Greenwood without trace. Running from those Fenians already initiated, they would have to duck beneath a branch knee-height and jump over one as high as their foreheads, pluck a thorn from their foot, all this without ever breaking their stride, and above all without leaving a trace of their passing. One broken branch, even a twig, would lead to their being unable to join these magical warriors. They had to match the legendary skills of the forest-dwellers still remembered in Irish Legend as the Firbolg.

Other familiar themes appear in the Fenian saga. Like Arthur, Finn is betrayed by his wife and favourite knight, Dermot, but like Robin and Rama he 'rescues' her. The love between Dermot and Finn is so strong, though, that while Finn plays chess beneath a tree in which Dermot is hiding, Dermot cannot bear to see Finn make a wrong move, and drops berries onto the correct piece to move next. Finn is also accompanied by a bard, Oisin his son, usually known as Ossian, and it is to this Alan-A-Dale that the huge volumes of Finn poems are usually attributed. The Bardic tradition remained powerful in Ireland until the time of Cromwell, and cannot truly be said to have ever really died, and it is this aspect that gives the Finn stories an interesting parallel with Robin.

The Irish Bards were divided into two classes. The Upper caste, the Fili, were the court poets, regaling the Celtic aristocrats with tales from an earlier cycle, that about the Red Branch warriors and their hero Cuchulainn. The Bards themselves were a lower class, and it was they who told the more populist tales of Finn. Indeed, eventually Finn became so popular that the aristocracy demanded to hear of him too, but in general the relationship between Fili and Bards was that of the Troubadours and the Minstrels. Modern Gaelic scholars have noted that the class distinction between the Red Branch cycle and the Fenian cycle was very similar to that between the Grail Romances and the Robin Hood legends. These were always poems, and perhaps it is not surprising that they made Finn, as well as his son, a Bard. Indeed, a certain amount of heroism was necessary to the bardic process, since the final test was to compose a verse while lying at the bottom of a river, breathing through a straw, for an entire night. Perhaps reflecting the Fenian training itself, all Bards were trained in Winter, only emerging at Spring to see again the forests and mountains of which they wrote. While the poems of Ossian were known from the furthest western reaches of Ireland to northernmost Scotland, it is revealing that only seasonal nature poetry is attributed to Finn himself, including a poem about Mayday. An excellent English verse translation, by Rolleston I reprint here because it not only gives an idea of the Maytime as seen

35

from the Irish Bardic perspective, but in translation has been made
to reproduce the internal rhymes and alliterations of Irish poetry:

The Song Of Finn In Praise Of May
(9th century)

May Day ! Delightful day!
Bright colours play the vales along.
Now wakes at morning's slender ray,
Wild and gay, the blackbird's song.

Now comes the bird of dusty hue,
The loud cuckoo, the summer-lover;
Branching trees are thick with leaves;
The bitter, evil time is over.

Swift horses gather nigh
Where half dry the river goes;
Tufted heather crowns the height;
Weak and white the bogdown blows.

Corncrake sings from eve till morn,
Deep in corn, a strenuous bard!
Sings the virgin waterfall,
White and tall, her one sweet word.

Loaded bees of little power,
Goodly flower-harvest win;
Cattle roam with muddy flanks;
Busy ants go out and in.

Through the wild harp of the wood
Making music roars the gale-
Now it slumbers without motion,
On the ocean sleeps the sail.

Men grow mighty in the May,
Proud and gay the maidens grow;
Fair is every wooded height;
Fair and bright the plain below.

A bright shaft has smit the streams,
With gold gleams the water-flag;
Leaps the fish, and on the hills
Ardour thrills the flying stag.

Carols loud the lark on high,
Small and shy, his tireless lay,
Singing in wildest, merriest mood
Of delicate-hued, delightful May.

The final tale of the saga seems so have parallels with that of
Rama. Just as the first telling of the tale of Rama is itself divine, so
the tragedy of Ossian is based upon the faery lore. Ossian meets a
beautiful maiden from Tir Na nOg, the land of eternal youth. They
fall in love and go to live in the blessed isles. After a while, Ossian
pines for Ireland and is allowed to ride back, but warned not to set
foot upon the earth. He rides through Ireland but is unable to find
any of the Fenians, nor anyone who remembers them. Stepping
from his horse to perform an act of kindness, he instantly ages and
spends his last years recounting the tales of his father and his merry
band.

That Finn would give to the poor was proverbial, and his
success in winning over Goll Of The Blows from the enemy to his

own side is highly similar to the story of Robin and Little John. What we have here is not so much a contributor to the tale of Robin as a parallel development. Nevertheless, there was no strict division between the worlds of the Brythons and Gaels. When Finn wins control over the Fenians he offers the errant leaders the chance to take up allegiance with foreign kings, including Arthur. While it is unlikely that the rural English would have heard of Finn directly, he was well loved in Scotland, and Scott himself would certainly have known of him, possibly taking material from the Ossianic cycle to include in the section in Ivanhoe devoted to Robin. And so another thread towards the weaving of the legend of Robin Hood can be discerned.

CHAPTER SIX

BOWSHOT!

THE longbow has a unique place in the history of England. Never has a ruling elite had to compromise so heavily with an oppressed population than did the Norman conquerors over the question of this magnificent weapon.

The significance of the bow is manifold, especially with regard to Robin Hood. His men used the longbow in spite of the existence of the Norman crossbow, a much more powerful weapon that has won the hearts of the Swiss. Their own rebel hero, William Tell, used it as skilfully against the Austrians as the Merry Men used their Saxon bows against the Normans.

Their can be no doubt that the Saxon/Norman conflict has a major part in the shaping of the legend. One of the main advantages of the longbow over the crossbow is its relative silence, the twang of a crossbow can be heard far away. This could alert the Rangers employed by the Normans to keep the Saxon population from 'poaching' the game that had until recently been theirs by right. However, the Eyre Rolls for Worcestershire in 1270 that record fines for poaching show that it was a widespread activity. It was not only poor peasants but the rural middle class, mainly of Saxon stock, who organised whole expeditions in the hope that they wouldn't be caught, or perhaps after bribing the Rangers. They may also have regarded the fines as an informal tax, though there are instances of clergymen bankrupting themselves after being caught too often. However, the evidence required by the courts was scanty, it seems to have been sufficient merely to describe someone as a well-known poacher, so a great deal of resentment must have grown up. The 1270 rolls show 54 people being fined a total of £157, at a time when the highest recorded annual tax paid by any of the offenders was a third of a pound. Many were too poor to pay more than a tenth, and indeed thirty more offenders were not fined. Several women were imprisoned for 'handling stolen venison'.

The fact, revealed by the Rolls, that the Rangers were unable to provide real proof, and could not even give an estimate of how many deer had been shot, implies that the silent longbow was very effective, even if its use simply led to remarkably unfair methods of enforcement.

The significance of the longbow became even greater after the battle of Crecy. The Welsh longbow, in the hands of peasant soldiers who would not have been able to afford a crossbow, was able to kill a fully armoured knight. Never before had the knights and their equally armoured horses been vulnerable to footsoldiers. They were the ancient equivalent of the tank, and were used to cutting a swathe through the opposing army to engage enemy knights in combat. The success of the longbow at Crecy did more than win a battle, it upset the entire feudal order. That the knights should actually be vulnerable to the peasantry destroyed the mentality of natural servitude upon which feudalism depended, demoralising the knights and heartening the peasants.

The heyday of the longbow in popular legend came with the battle of Agincourt where, as every English schoolboy once knew, the Saxon yeoman archers defeated 'The Flower Of French Chivalry'. The re-creation of that moment is an abiding memory for those of us who have seen the late Sir Laurence Olivier, ironically of French Huguenot stock, leading his men, once more, into the breach. This, and other victories, lead to a particular English affinity with the bow, and in the mediaeval period it was compulsory for every male over the age of seven to posses a longbow equal to their own height, and to practise with it for four hours on a Sunday. Legend persists that this law has never actually been repealed, although in fact it has been removed from law by general Acts of the sort that replace whole groups of earlier statutes. It would seem that the legend of Robin soon managed to link these practices with Mayday. Henry VIII, who was certainly fond of Mayday, was famed as an archer, as Holinshed mentions in his history of the King:

'On the May-day then next following, the second year of his reign, his grace being young, and willing not to be idle, rose in the morning very early, to fetch May, or green boughs; himself fresh and richly appareled and clothed, all his knights, squires, and gentlemen in white satin, and all his guard and yeomen of the crown in white sacenet; and so went every man with his bow and arrows shooting to the wood, and so returning again to the court, every man with a green bough in his cap. Now at his returning, many hearing of his going a maying, were desirous to see him shoot, for at that time his grace shot as strong and as a great a length as any of his guards. There came to his grace a certain man with bows and arrows, and desired his grace to take the muster of him, and to see him shoot; for at that time his grace was contented. The man put then one foot in his bosom, and so did shoot, and shot a very good shot, and well towards his mark; whereof not only his grace, but all others greatly marvelled. So the king gave him a reward for his so doing, which person after of the people and of those in the court was called, Foot-In-Bosom.'

We shall see later that such jocular Mayday archery was an essential part of the growth of the legend of Robin. But the legend created by the very real Agincourt was to have a spooky sequel during the First World War at the Battle of Mons.

Arthur Machen, justly regarded as one of the best ever Welsh writers, and certainly one the greatest British writers of the supernatural, is mainly remembered nowadays for his great short novels. A member of the esoteric Hermetic Order Of The Golden Dawn, he too told of phantom archers hiding in the Welsh wilds, descended from ancient Mesolithic peoples. However, his greatest moment came as a creator of uncanny 'fact'. At the height of the battle of Mons he wrote a very short story called, simply, The Bowmen, which was published on the front page of a popular newspaper. This told of a phantom army of bowmen, the ghosts of the archers of Agincourt, appearing in the clouds at the battle of Mons, cutting down the German hordes with what became very real arrows. This piece of patriotic whimsy was by no means his best work. It was written to get some money, and very little ever came to him during his lifetime, indeed, a first edition of any one of his works can fetch more nowadays than he ever earned during his lifetime. Nevertheless, his short piece was to haunt him for the rest of his life.

When the Battle of Mons was over, and survivors began to return to Britain, again and again they gave eyewitness accounts of seeing the 'Angels Of Mons', phantom archers in the clouds, just as in Machen's short story. Even when confronted with the evidence of the newspaper story, clearly identified and written as a fictional piece, and not at all in the style of a newspaper report, they insisted that, nevertheless, they had seen this with their own eyes. If accused of lying they would be very angry, and this was repeated all over the country. The Occult Review, a periodical that was able to appear monthly even during the War, regularly published accounts under such headlines as:

"The Angelic Leaders: Evidence from the Wounded at the Front" (August 1916)

In October, 1915, the main editorial article reported that Machen himself had been contacted by a Lieutenant Colonel who reported:

"On the night of the 27th (of August, 1914) I was riding along in the column with two other officers.....I became conscious of the fact that in the fields....I could see a very large body of horsemen."

Later many of his column verified the apparition. Another soldier reported:

"I could see quite plainly in mid-air a strange light....I could see quite distinctly three shapes, one in the centre having what looked like outspread wings......I am not a believer in such things."

Before long, the legend of the Angels Of Mons had become a part of British folklore that still leaves experts on such matters puzzled. Some have gone so far as to suggest that the event was in some ways real, and either intuited by Machen or even, give his experience in a magical order, somehow created by him.

However spectacular this may be, there is an esoteric significance to the bow that goes right back to the Neolithic period in the form of the bowshot. 'A bowshot' was once a unit of measurement, originally calculated by the literal shooting of an arrow. This was used to determine limits and boundaries, and was preferred because of the significance of the straightness of the flight of an arrow. One of the many legends of the founding of Salisbury cathedral tells of Bishop Poore, who shot an arrow from the original site at Old Sarum, and the new site was the point where the arrow fell. Old Sarum, Stonehenge and Salisbury Cathedral lie on the 'Old Sarum Ley', and the 14th Century church of St Tegai in Wales was founded 'two bowshots away' from a now forgotten site. It is worth noting, then, that the old ballads attribute to both Robin and Little John the ability to shoot precisely a measured mile, while Robin's father had the strange feat to his credit of shooting two miles and one inch.

The sacred nature of straightness dates from at least the Neolithic period. I will not go over all of the research into the alignment of sacred sites, but it has been well established that all over the world the holiness of the straight is a consistent feature. It is only in Britain that the Archaeological establishment has resisted this realisation, no doubt because Alfred Watkins, discoverer of the 'Ley Line', was an outsider to the world of professional academia. This position is at last changing, probably helped by the scientific-sounding phrase 'terrain oblivious alignment' that helps remove the concept from thoughts of Dowsers, UFO fanatics and the like, who have colonised the Ley Line concept to a large degree.

The holiness of the straight probably comes from a time when straightness was a very rare sight. In the Mesolithic world, the only straight feature that was not man-made was the ray of sunlight, seen breaking through the clouds. Thus the holiness associated with the sun, and perhaps the moonbeam too, became associated with the straight line, and one thing that had to be as straight as possible was the shaft of an arrow. To this day poets speak of the fiery arrows of the sun, occasionally shortened to darts, which originated as throwing arrows carried by archers for short-range combat. This is, of course, the origin of the slang term 'arrows' used in the game of darts. The dartboard, not surprisingly, was originally a cut cross-section of a tree, as was the archery target that Robin could hit so accurately.

It is at the moment of the death of Robin Hood that the sacred bowshot comes into its own. As we all know, as he lay dying he asked for his bow to be brought to him, fired an arrow into the Greenwood and asked to be buried where it landed. Chapter Eight reprints an ancient ballad on this moment. The arrow became a symbol for his spirit, flying back to its place of origin to indicate the precise spot where he could again be at one with the forest. The next time you hear an American using the phrase 'straight arrow' to mean 'it's true, honestly', you are hearing a hint of an idea that, whether the phrase itself comes from old English or Native American usage, comes from the birth of history.

CHAPTER SEVEN

THE MAYDAY ROBIN
AND THE MORRIS DANCE

IN various books attempting to 'find' the real Robin Hood, occasional mention is made of his connection with Mayday festivities, but this is always assumed to be a later invention. His role in the Morris is something else, but the two are so closely connected it is impossible to separate them.

I have stated that the battles with King John and his Sheriff are useful to explain away pagan festivals. These are the Mayday festivities and those of May in general, including those at Whitsun. Mayday is not itself a typically Celtic or Saxon observance, though it has become so. The connection is with Rome. Floralia, the festival of the Goddess Flora, was celebrated on May 1, and although the Celts may have celebrated it, it does not fall onto one of the dates of their sacred calendar. Rather, Floralia was so popular that the Roman Church could not only not abolish it, they Christianised it to the point that they took it with them to Ireland, where it is now an insipid and sterile custom associated with virginity. However, its popularity, even in a castrated form, spread it throughout Europe.

English Mayday was something else entirely. The modern, twee descendants of the older, enormous, phallic Maypoles of the past are nowadays lucky to reach 20 ft in height, but once poles over a hundred feet in height were not uncommon. They were, in fact, tall trees, stripped of their branches, and are connected with the many 'one tree' hills still found all over England, referring to the ancient custom of forest-clearers where the central tree of the tallest hill would be left to stand. This was itself an acknowledgement of the fertility of the greenwood, a final tribute to the most powerful of the trees. It was also rather a good look-out post!

It would be inconceivable, then, for Robin not to be involved, and indeed he was. The evidence suggests that his connection diminished with time where other aspects grew. It is clear that modern revivals of Mayday festivities have ignored him, perhaps for fear that he was a late intrusion, or because his presence was made unwelcome by a church always eager to contain and sterilise what it could not abolish. The following account is from the 18th Century novel 'Queen Hoo Hall', recounting the events of earlier centuries, and gives a fair idea of the normal course of events before the Reformation:

'In the front of the pavilion, a large square was staked out, and fenced with ropes, to prevent the crowd from pressing upon the performers, and interrupting the division; there were also two bars at the bottom of the enclosure, through which the actors might part and repass, as occasion required. Six young men first entered the square, clothed in jerkins of leather, with axes upon their shoulders like woodmen, and their heads bound with large garlands of ivy leaves, intertwined with sprigs of hawthorn. Then followed six young maidens of the village, dressed in blue kirtles, with garlands of primroses on their heads, leading a fine sleek cow decorated with ribbons of various colours interspersed with flowers; and the horns of the animal were tipped with gold. These were succeeded by six foresters equipped in green tunics, with hoods and hosen of the same colour; each of them carried a bugle- horn attached to a baldrick of silk, which he sounded as he passed the barrier. After them came Peter Lanaret, the baron's chief falconer, who personified Robin Hood; he was attired in a bright grass-green tunic, fringed with gold; his hood and his hosen were parti-coloured, blue and white; he had a large garland of rosebuds on his head, a bow bent in his hand, a sheaf of arrows at his girdle, and a bugle-horn depending from a baldrick of light blue tarantine, embroidered with silver; he had also a sword and a dagger, the hilts of both being richly embossed with gold. Fabian, a page, as Little John, walked at his right hand; and Cecil Cellerman, the butler, as Will Stukely, at his left. These, with ten others of the jolly outlaw's attendants who followed, were habited in green garments, bearing their bows bent in their hands, and their arrows in their girdles. Then came two maidens, in orange-coloured kirtles with white courtpies, strewing flowers, followed immediately by the Maid Marian, elegantly habited in a watchet-coloured tunic reaching to the ground. She was supported by two bride-maidens, in sky-coloured rochets girt with crimson girdles. After them came four other females in green courtpies, and garlands of violets and cowslips. Then Sampson, the smith, as Friar Tuck, carrying a huge quarter-staff on his shoulder; and Morris, the mole-taker, who represented Much The Miller's Son, having a long pole with an inflated bladder attached to one end. And after them the May-pole, drawn by eight fine oxen, decorated with scarfs, ribbons, and flowers of divers colours, and the tips of their horns were embellished with gold. The rear was closed by the hobby-horse and the dragon.

When the May-pole was drawn into the square, the foresters sounded their horns, and the populace expressed their pleasure by shouting incessantly until it reached the place assigned for its elevation. During the time the ground was preparing for its reception, the barriers of the bottom of the enclosure were opened for the villagers to approach and adorn it with ribbons, garlands, and flowers, as their inclination prompted them. The pole being sufficiently onerated with finery, the square was cleared from such as had no part to perform in the pageant, and then it was elevated amidst the reiterated acclamations of the spectators. The woodmen and the milk-maidens danced around it according to the rustic fashion; and the measure was played by Peretto Cheveritte, the baron's chief minstrel, on the bagpipes, accompanied with the pipe and tabor, performed by one of his associates. When the dance was finished, Gregory the jester, who undertook to play the hobby-horse, came forward with his appropriate equipment, and frisking up and down the square without restriction, imitated the galloping, curvetting, ambling, trotting, and other paces of a horse, to the infinite satisfaction of the lower classes of the spectators. He was followed by Peter Parker, the baron's ranger, who personated a dragon, hissing, yelling, and shaking his wings with wonderful ingenuity; and to complete the mirth, Morris, in the character of Much, having small bells attached to his knees and elbows, capered here and there between the two monsters in the form of a dance; and as often as he came near to the sides of the enclosure, he cast slyly a handful of meal into the faces of the gaping rustics, or rapped them about their heads with the bladder tied at the end of his pole. In the meantime Sampson, representing Friar Tuck, walked with much gravity around the square, and occasionally let fall his heavy staff upon the toes of such of the crowd as he thought were approaching more forward than they ought to do; and if the sufferers cried out from the sense of pain, he addressed them in a solemn tone of voice, advising them to count their beads, say a paternoster or two, and to beware of purgatory. These vagaries were highly palatable to the populace, who announced their delight by repeated plaudits and loud bursts of laughter; for this reason they were continued for a considerable length of time; but Gregory, beginning at last to falter in his paces, ordered the dragon to fall back. The well-nurtured beast, being out of breath, readily obeyed, and their two companions followed their example, which concluded this part of the pastime. Then the archers set up a target at the lower part of the green, and made trial of their skill in a regular succession. Robin Hood and Will Stukely excelled their comrades, and both of them lodged an arrow in the centre circle of gold, so near to each other that the difference could not readily be decided, which occasioned them to shoot again, when Robin struck the gold a second time, and Stukeley's arrow was affixed upon the edge of it. Robin was therefore adjudged the conqueror; and the prize of honour, a garland of laurel embellished with variegated ribbons, was put upon his head; and to Stukely was given a garland of ivy; because he was the second best performer in that contest. The pageant was finished with the archery, and the procession began to move away to make room for the villagers, who afterwards amused themselves by dancing around the May-pole in promiscuous companies, according to the ancient custom.'

These events bear a remarkable resemblance to modern Hindu festivities, particularly with the decorated cow and the dancing milkmaids, sacred to Krishna. The costume of Maid Marian is evidently that of flowers rather than the green foliage that decorates the men, suggesting that the modern habit of portraying her as 'one of the boys' is mistaken. The creation of a special space, within which only the performers may walk during the festival, is further evidence of pagan survival, as is the ritual horn-blowing. It is evident that the one feature that is missing here, that of a Queen of the May, is represented by Marian herself. This may be because the term is Scottish. The following extract from the Book Of Days of 1878 both suggests and confuses the connection:

'In Scotland, the Robin Hood games were enacted with great vivacity at various places, but particularly at Edinburgh; and in connection with them were the sports of the Abbot Of Unreason, a strange half serious burlesque on some of the ecclesiastical arrangements then prevalent, and also a representation called the Queen of May. A recent historical work, the Domestic Annals of Scotland, thus describes what took place at these whimsical merry-makings: 'At the approach of May, they (the people) assembled and chose some respectable individuals of their number - very grave and reverend citizens, perhaps - to act the parts of Robin Hood and Little John, of the Lord of Inobedience or the Abbot of Unreason, and "make sports and jocosoties" for them. If the chosen actors felt it inconsistent with their tastes, gravity, or engagements, to don a fantastic dress, caper and dance, and incite their neighbours to do the like, they could only be excused on paying a fine. On the appointed day, always a Sunday or holiday, the people assembled in their best attire and in military array, and marched in blithe procession to some neighbouring field, where the fitting preparations had been made for their amusement. Robin Hood and Little John robbed bishops, fought with pinners, and contended in archery among themselves, as they had done in reality two centuries before. The Abbot of Unreason kicked up his heels and played antics, like a modern pantaloon.' Maid Marian also appeared upon the scene, in flower-sprent kirtle, and with bows and arrows in hand, and doubtless slew hearts as she had formerly done harts. Mingling with the mad scene were the morris-dancers, with their fantastic dresses and jingling bells. So it was until the Reformation, when a sudden stop was put to the whole affair by severe penalties imposed by Act of Parliament.'

It is unclear here whether Marian was the Queen of May, but what is evident is that there are many differences between the English and Scottish Maydays, yet both involved Robin Hood, Marian, Little John and an archery contest. Other recognisable pagan elements are here too, the Lord of Misrule descends, not from Floralia, but Saturnalia, when all roles were reversed, the lowest becoming highest.

The Queen Hoo story reminds us that these celebrations were not merely confined to the peasantry, since the entire affair had been paid for by the Baron. Indeed, it is known that King Henry VIII and his first wife, Catherine of Aragon, participated in such revels at Oxleas Wood on top of Shooters' Hill, only a mile from Charlton House. The final chapter contains more about Oxleas Woods. It is from events like this that we can see the role of Marian. Maid Marian is, simply, May Marian, the Mary of May and thus a Christianised Flora. She represents the fertility associated with spring and symbolised by flowers. We can also see here the development of the rather twee costumes associated with Robin and his band, as reflected in the films of Errol Flynn, the TV series starring Richard Greene (what an appropriate surname) and satirized by John Cleese in Terry Gilliams' 'Time Bandits'. It is Marian who was once bound to the Maypole by the ribbons held by the revellers. Strangely enough, it was also she who danced with Robin in the Morris dance, and it to this that we now turn.

Morris dancing is a comparatively recent addition to the Robin saga, since it only dates back to the time of the Crusades. The following extract from the Day Book shows the theories prevalent in the 19th century, when it was still vigorous and not yet a revival.

'Antiquaries seem agreed that the old English morris-dance, so great a favourite in this country in the sixteenth century, was derived through Spain from the Moors, and that its name, in Spanish Morisco, a Moor, was taken from this circumstance. It has been supposed to be originally identified with the fandango. It was certainly popular in France as early as the fifteenth century, under the name of Morisque, which is an intermediate step between the Spanish Morisco and the English Morris. We are not aware of any mention of this dance in English writers or records before the sixteenth century; but then, and especially in writers of the Shakespearian age, the allusions to it become very numerous. It was probably introduced into this country by dancrs both from Sain and France, for in the earlier allusions to it in English it is sometimes called the Morisco, and sometimes the Morisce or Morisk. Here, however, it seems to have been very soon united with an older pageant dance, performed at certain periods in honour of Robin Hood and his outlaws, and thus a morris-dance consisted of a certain number or characters, limited at one time to five, but varying considerably at different periods. The earliest allusions to the morris-dance and its characters were found by Mr Lysons in the churchwardens' and chamberlains' books at Kingston-upon-Thames, and range through the last two years of the reign of Henry VII, and the greater part of that of his successor, Henry VIII. We learn that the two principal characters in the dance represented Robin Hood and Maid Marian; and the various expenses connected with their different articles of dress, show that they were decked out very gaily. There was also a frere, or friar; a musician, who is sometimes called a minstrel, sometimes a piper, and at others a taborer,- in fact he was a performer on the pipe and tabor, and a 'dysard' or fool. The churchwardens accounts of St. Mary's, Reading, for 1557, add to these characters that of the hobby-horse. 'Item, payed to the mynstrels and the hobby-horse uppon May-day, 3s.' Payments to the morris-dancers are again recorded on the Sunday after Mayday, and at Whitsuntide. The dancers, perhaps, at first represented Moors - prototypes of the Ethiopian minstrels of the present day, or at least there was one moor among them; and small bells, usually attached to their legs, were indispensable to them. In the Kingston accounts of the 29th of Henry VIII (1537-8), the wardrobe of the morris-dancers, then in the custody of the church-wardens, is thus enumerated:- A fryers cote of russet, and a kyrtele weltyd with red cloth, a Mowrens (Moor's) cote of buckram, and four morres daunsars cotes of white fustian spangelid, and too gryne saten cotes, and disarddes cote of cotton, and six payre of garters with belles.'

However, Morris dancing was supposed to be an exclusively male pastime, more suited to the athletics field than the dance floor. That it has a 'moorish' history may well explain, or be explained away by, the dark faces of mummers, some Morris troops and the 'sweeps' of Rochester who still carry out these ancient dances. Note that one moor at least was part of the Robin Hood Morris; when the character of Nazir the Assassin appeared in 'Robin Of Sherwood' there was criticism that this person had been introduced by Richard Carpenter without any justification. We can now see that his presence was fully justified, far more so than the American accents in 'Robin Hood, Prince of Thieves'! Women did dance in traditional measures in what was known, in contrast to the male Morris, as Contray Dancing, meaning Opposite, since the women danced in lines opposite lines of men. The Anglo-Norman Contray has nowadays been corrupted into Country, and the steps are varied, as opposed to the exhausting 'hop' step of the Morris. However, the possibility that women did once dance as Marian, using the tiring steps, is suggested from the following extract from the journal of William Kemp, whose famous dance from London to Norwich in

1599 included this charming little episode, recounted in the then famous pamphlet 'Kemp's nine daies wonder' printed the next year:

'In this towne of Sudbury there came a lusty, tall fellow, a butcher by his profession, that would in a Morrice keepe me company to Bury. I being glad of his friendly offer, gave him thankes, and forward wee did set; but ere ever wee had measur'd halfe a mile of our way, he gave me over in the plain field, protesting, that if he might get a 100 pound, he would not hold out with me; for, indeed, my pace in dancing is not ordinary. As he and I wee parting, a lusty country lasse being among the people, cal'd him faint-hearted lout, saying, "If I had begun to daunce, I would had held out one myle, though it had cost my life." At which words many laughed. "Nay," sayeth she, "if the dauncer will lend me a leash of his belles, I'le venter to treade one myle wit him myselfe." I lookt upon her, saw mirth in her eies, heard boldness in her words, and beheld her ready to tucke up her russat petticoate; I fitted her with bels, which she merrily taking, garnisht her thicke short legs, and with a smooth brow bad the tabrer begin. The drum stricke; forward marcht I with my merry Mayde Marian, who shooke her fat sides, and footed it merrily to Melford, being a long myle. There parting with her (besides her skinfull of drinke), and English crowne to buy more drinke; for, good wench, she was in a piteous heate; my kindness she requited with dropping some dozen of short courtsies, and bidding God blesse the dauncer. I bade her adieu; and, to give her her due, she had a good eare, daunst truly, and wee parted friends.'

We cannot say for sure that the steps of this dance were the modern Morris steps, but it seems likely given the apparently exhausting nature of the event. In later times, when Morris dancing had thrown up various different dances, becoming mixed in with stick dances, sword dances and the like, the role of Marian was played by a man, often extremely ugly and bearded, and the name itself fell from usage.

Finally, in case it seems that my theories are rather modern, this account from the Day Book makes it clear that the pagan connections have been common knowledge for some time:

'There was preserved in an ancient mansion at Betley, in Staffordshire, some years ago, and we suppose that it exists there still, a painted glass window of apparently the reign of Henry VIII, representing in its different compartments the several characters of the morris-dance. George Tollett, Esq, who possessed the mansion at the beginning of this (19th) century, and who was a friend of the Shakespearian critic, Malone, gave a rather lengthy dissertation on this window, with an engraving, in the variorum edition of the works of Shakspeare. Maid Marian, the queen of May, is there dressed in a rich costume of the period referred to, with a golden crown on her head, and a red pink, supposed to be intended as the emblem of summer, in her left hand. This queen of May is supposed to represent the goddess Flora of the Roman festival; Robin Hood appears as the lover of Maid Marian. An ecclesiastic also appears among the characters in the window, in the full clerical tonsure, with a chaplet of white and red beads in his right hand, his corded girdle and his russet habit denoting him to be of the Franciscan order, or one of the Grey friars; his stocking are red; his red girdle is ornamented with a golden twist, and with a golden tassle. This is supposed to be Friar Tuck, a well-known character of the Robin Hood Ballads. The fool, with his cocks' comb and bauble, also takes his place in the window; nor are the tabourer, with his tabor and pipe, or the hobby-horse wanting.'

This long accepted link between Robin and Mayday brings us to another character often associated with the development of the Robin myth, that of Jack-in-the-green. He too was represented at Mayday festivities, where he appears as a man dressed entirely in green foliage, often supported on a frame covered in boughs so as to make him appear totally inhuman. His legend is that he was originally Melvas, the King of Somerset in the days of King Arthur.

At Mayday he lay in wait for Guinevere as she went 'maying', disguised in green boughs. He was discovered and condemned to a life in the woods, always dressed in green. This story was enacted with the Mayday festivities, and it is obvious that here we have a fertility ritual, accompanied with an Arthurian just-so story. This ceremony too involved sweeps, and a modern play for children by Violet M.Methley ingeniously links this story with that of Charles II, whose habit of hiding in oak trees has been mentioned. Here the mayers hide Charles from the puritans in the Jack-in-the-Green frame, thus giving Charles a role that we have already traced back to prehistory, that of the unjustly disinherited king hiding in the greenwood until his time to return comes around at last. Strangely enough, it was hatred of his younger brother, James II, that led to the bloodless Glorious Revolution. Some roles, it would seem, repeat themselves in real history as much as they do in mythology, and the legend that James II threw the Great Seal into the Thames can be traced back to John losing the crown jewels in the Wash, regardless of whether neither, either or both of these events actually happened.

So the Mayday festivities, with dancers and archery, represent, through Robin and Marian and associated figures, both masculine prowess and feminine fertility. The ritual of the maypole represents impregnation. This connection can be seen in the tale of Rama, where Sita is discovered in the furrow left by a plough moments later. Moreover, at Maytide the dance represented the raw power of the forest brought out before the people. The final chapter presents a modern equivalent of this concept from Africa.

It is at this point that the naming of Robin's band becomes interesting. We can see that the dancers represent characters from the Robin Hood legend, but it would be wrong to assume that the legend, including their names, came first. A little look at phallic slang is revealing.

Ross Nichols, Chosen Chief of the Order Of Bards, Ovates and Druids from 1964-1975, discovered that Robin was once slang for penis. As such, the Hood becomes significant. It explains why Hood, rather than Hob, Hobby or Hooden, became the fixed form of the name. Other first names for men have become slang for the same part of the anatomy over the years, so that we have the Hooded Robin leading a band including John, who may be called Little but is actually very big; Will, who is apparently Scarle; and a monk called Friar Tuck who, by transposing the first letter of each part of his name, becomes a suggestion that meant exactly the same thing hundreds of years ago that it does today. In the older ballads and games, Will Scarlet was Will Stukely or Scathlock and Friar Tuck was Friar Carey. If this sounds far-fetched, understand that it would be typically earthy, rustic humour to name the men enacting the ritual impregnation of the *May Marian* with such titles. It certainly explains why some of the names changed while others did not. Sometimes later corruptions can be as revealing as original, 'authentic' names.

So, from lore as old as time itself, we gather a nice, convincing explanation of the origin of the May celebrations, one that will satisfy children and vicars but leave the true meaning safely in the hands of those who had kept the tradition alive through centuries of Christian persecution. The peasants jokingly re-named characters or developed new slang terms from them, certainly 'Robin' is an older term than the slang usage, so that they would be reminded of the fertility aspects of the festivities.

CHAPTER EIGHT

FROM MINSTREL SONG TO MOVIE SCRIPT

WHATEVER else the tale of Robin Hood may be, it is certainly a myth, and it is a myth that is still developing today. It is interesting to note now, not so much who the myth may be about, or who heard it, but who it was that developed it.

The earliest tales of Robin Hood come in the form of minstrel ballads. Some of the most famous, such as "The Little Geste of Robin Hoode" and "Robin Hood and Little John" have been reprinted many times, so I have decided to reprint lesser known works. The minstrels themselves give important clues as to the reason that the story of Robin developed such archetypal themes. The world of mediaeval England was sharply divided socially, and so were its entertainers. There has been much fascinating research into the nature of the Troubadours and the Cult of Courtly Love, which I can only summarize here. They were of French and Norman origin, although the movement spread into Italy and Germany, where later the Meistersingers and Minnesingers held sway. They sang of love, but a new concept of love that continues to haunt our society. This is romantic love, named for the Romance languages in which they were written.

Essential to the Troubadour mythos is the unattainable woman. The perfect, gentle knight must woo her without hope of physical satisfaction, though it was understood that if he did really well he might just, like Lancelot with Guinevere, get lucky. This perfect woman was usually unattainable because she was married to

57

somebody else, and the origin of the success of this theme seems to be in the unfairness of the rules of the feudal system whereby the eldest son inherited everything. This meant that, as far as a noble father was concerned, only eldest sons made suitable suitors for their daughters. A s a result Europe was flooded with highly trained noblemen without land or lady, listening with a sigh to the song of the Troubadour and deciding to either go off on a Crusade, or woo the wife of an eldest son while *he* was away on a crusade. This is, of course, what John did, though he seems to have preferred the wives of millers (see above).

The essential framework of the Troubadour songs was the Grail romances. The Grail, supposedly the cup used at the last supper, itself became a symbol, and a noticeably feminine one, for that only attainable by the purest and best. It seems to be related to the cauldron of Cerridwen, itself linked to the Cornucopia mentioned in the tale of the Charlton Horn Fair. The Church was naturally a bit suspicious about this, and there is plenty of evidence that the Courtly Love tradition inherited various heretical concepts from Gnostic and Pelagian sources, Pelagianism being an early heresy originating in Wales. The most persistent heresies were always those that elevated women above that lowly status accorded her by a church which, towards the end of the first millenium, was capable of convening a special synod to determine whether or not women were really human beings.

In the everyday world of the peasantry, the longing for the feminine side of divinity was expressed in the cult of the Virgin Mary. The Church tried as hard as possible to control the cult, since it was obvious to them that she was being treated much as a pagan Goddess, indeed the phrase 'Mother Of God' was only accepted in the 19th Century, against much clerical opposition. And in the everyday life of the peasants of England the bardic role was played by the Minstrels. If Troubadours were the Rock Stars of the Mediaeval period, as is occasionally stated, then the minstrels were the stand-up comedians, and their tales were not of the Grail but of the various misdemeanours of the Nobility, of ancient Celtic kings, and of Robin Hood. One such ballad relates to a figure much associated with Robin Hood, and this is the enigmatic Robin Goodfellow, who is the character called 'Puck' in A Midsummer Night's Dream (the name is the same as that of the even more rumbustious 'Pookah', as seen in the James Stewart film 'Harvey'). This is a mischievous fellow who steals in from the woods to play pranks upon the locals, but he is never vicious, and this ancient ballad gives an idea of this forest spirit at his best:

ROBIN GOODFELLOW

From Oberon in fairye land,
The king of ghosts and shadowes there,
Mad Robin I, at his command,
Am sent to viewe the night sports here.
What revell rout
Is kept about,
In every corner where I go,
I will o'ersee, and merry bee,
And make good sport, with ho, ho, ho!

More swift than lightening can I flye
About this aery welkin soone,

And, in a minutes space, descrye
Each thing that's done belowe the moone,
There's not a hag
Or ghost shall wag,
Or cry, ware Goblins! where I go;
But Robin I their feates will spy,
And send them home, with ho, ho, ho!

Whene'er such wanderers I meete,
As from their night-sports they trudge home;
With counterfeiting voice I greete,
And call them on, with me to roame
Thro' woods, thro' lakes,
Thro;' bogs, thro' brakes;
Or else, unseene, with them I go,
All in the nicke to play some tricke
And frolicke it, with ho, ho, ho!

Sometimes I meete them like a man;
Sometimes, an ox, sometimes, a hound;
And to a horse I turn mecan;
To trip and trot about them round.
But if, to ride,
My backe they stride,
More swift than winde away I go,
Ore hedge and lands, thro' pools and ponds
I whirry, laughing, ho, ho, ho!

When lads and lasses merry be,
With possets and with juncates fine,
Unseene of all the company,
I eat their cakes and sip their wine;
And to make sport,
II snore and snort;
And out the candles I do blow:
The maids I kiss; they shrieke - Who's this?
I answer naught, but ho, ho, ho!

Yet now and then, the maids to please,
At midnight I card up their woll;
And while they sleepe and take their ease,
With wheel, to threads, their flax I pull.
I grind at mill
Their malt up still;
I dress their hemp, I spen their tow:
If any 'wake, and woulde me take,
I wend me, laughing, ho, ho, ho!

When house or harth doth sluttish lye,
I pinch their maidens black and blue;
The bed-clothes from the bedd pull I
And lay them naked all to view.
'Twixt sleepe and wake,
I do them take,
And on the key-cold floor them throw.
If out they cry, then forth I fly,
And loudly laugh out, ho, ho, ho!

When any need to borrowe aught,
We lend them what they do require;
And for the use demand we nought:
Our owne is all we do desire.
If to repay,
They do delay,
Abroad amongst them then I go,
And night by night, I them affright
With pinchings, dreames, and ho, ho, ho!

When lazie queans have nought to do,
But study how to cog and lye;
To make debate and mischief too,
'Twixt one another secretlye:
I mark their gloze,
And it disclose,
To them whom they have wronged so;
When I have done, I get me gone,
And leave them scolding, ho, ho, ho!

When men do traps and engines set
In loope holes were the vermin creepe,
Who from their foldes and houses, get
Their duckes and geese, and lambes and
sheepe:
I spy the gin,
And enter in,
And seeme a vermine taken so;
But when they there approach me neare,
I leap out laughing, ho, ho, ho!

By walls and rills, in meadowes greene,
We nightly dance our hey-day guise;
And to our fairye king and queene
We chant our moon-light minstrelsies.
When larks gin sing,
Away we fling,
And babes new borne steale as we go,
And elfe in bed we leave instead,
And wend us laughing, ho, ho, ho!

From hag-bred Merlin's time have I
Thus nightly revelled to and fro;
And for my pranks men call me by
The name of Robin Good-fellow.
Fiends, ghosts, and sprites,
Who haunt the nights,
The hags and goblins do me know;
And beldames old my feates have told;
So Vale, Vale, ho, ho, ho!

Minstrels were more or less vagabonds, going from Tavern to Inn with their rougher verses. Their songs may have lacked the finer points of metre and rhyme, but if they were good they were popular. Like many a club comedian they had no qualms about stealing other peoples' material, and thus the best verses were passed throughout the land. It is no surprise that Robin, the noble yeoman who, in the recorded ballads, was only later to become a dispossessed nobleman, was a popular subject. The Saxon/Celtic peasantry was abominably treated by the Norman overlords, who failed to extend the concept of 'Our People' to the lower orders. This was inconceivable in Saxon or Celtic times, and those poor unfortunates who had lost an ear merely for hunting in the wrong place were ready to lend the remaining one to a good tale about a Sheriff being bettered by a crafty commoner. These next two ballads show first an encounter with Guy of Gisborne, and secondly the tragic death of our hero:

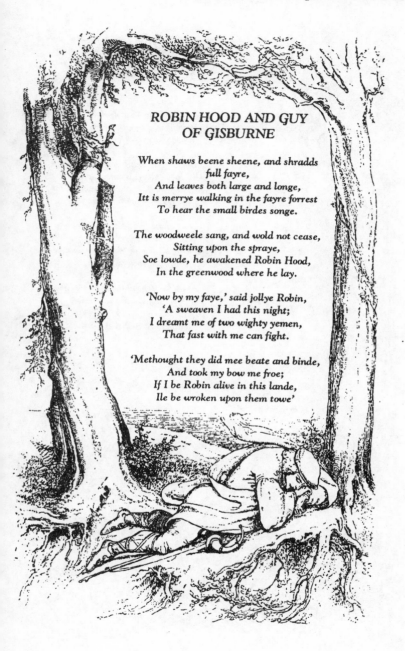

ROBIN HOOD AND GUY
OF GISBURNE

When shaws beene sheene, and shradds
full fayre,
And leaves both large and longe,
Itt is merrye walking in the fayre forrest
To hear the small birdes songe.

The woodweele sang, and wold not cease,
Sitting upon the spraye,
Soe lowde, he awakened Robin Hood,
In the greenwood where he lay.

'Now by my faye,' said jollye Robin,
'A sweaven I had this night;
I dreamt me of two wighty yemen,
That fast with me can fight.

'Methought they did mee beate and binde,
And took my bow me froe;
If I be Robin alive in this lande,
Ile be wroken upon them towe'

'Sweavens are swifte, master,' quoth John,
'As the wind that blowes ore a hill;
For if itt be never so loude this night,
To morrow itt may be still.'

'Buske yee, bowne yee, my merry men all,
And John shall goe with mee,
For Ile goe seeke yond wight yeomen,
In greenwood where the bee.'

The the cast on their gownes of grene,
And tooke theyr bowes each one;
And they away to the greene forrest
A shooting forth are gone.

Until they came to the merry greenwood,
Where they had gladdest bee,
Theye were the ware of a wights yeoman,
His body leaned to a tree.

A sword and a dagger he wore by his side,
Of manye a man the bane;
And he was clad in his capull hyde
Topp and tayll and mayne.

Robin Hood: The Spirit of the Forest

'Stand you still, master,' quoth Little John,
  'Under this tree so grene;
And I will go to yond wight yeoman
  To know what he doth meane.'

'Ah! John, by me thou settest noe store,
  And that I farley finde:
How offt send I my men beffore,
  And tarry my selfe behinde?

'It is no cunning a knave to ken,
  And a man but heare him speake;
And itt were not for bursting of my bowe,
  John, I thy head would breake.'

As often words they breeden bale,
  So they parted Robin and John;
And John is gone to Barnesdale:
  The gates he knoweth each one.

But when he came to Barnesdale,
  Great heaviness there hee hadd,
For he found tow of his owne fellowes,
  Were slaine both in a slade.

And Scarlette he was flying a-foote
  Fast over stocke and stone,
For the sheriffe with seven score men
  Fast after him is gone.

'One shoote now I will shoote,' quoth John,
  With Christ his might and mayne;
'Ile make yond fellow that flyes soe fast,
  To stopp he shall be fayne,'

Then John bent up his long bende-bow,
  And fetteled him to shoote:
The bow was made of a tender boughe,
  And fell downe to his foote.

'Woe worth, woe worth thee, wicked wood,
  That ere thou grew on a tree;
For now this day thou art my bale,
  My boote when thou shold bee.'

His shoote it was but loosely shott,
Yet flewe not the arrowe in vaine;
For itt mett one of the sheriffes men,
Good William a Trent was slaine.

It had bene better of William a Trent
To have bene abed with sorrowe,
Than to be that day in the green wood slade
To meet with Little John's arrowe.

But as it is said, when men be mett,
Fyve can doe more than three,
The sheriffe hath taken Little John,
And bound him fast to a tree.

'Thou shalt be drawen by dale and downe,
And hanged hye on a hill.'
'But thou mayst fayle of thy purpose,' quoth John,
'If itt be Christ his will.'

Let us leave talking of Little John,
And thinke of Robin Hood,
How he is gone to the wight yeoman,
Where under the leaves he stood.

'Good morrowe, good fellowe,' said Robin so fayre,
'Good morrowe, good fellowe,' quoth he:
'Methinkes by this bowe thou bears in thy hande
A good archere thou shouldst bee.'

'I am wilfull of my waye,' quo' the yeman,
'And of my morning tyde.'
'Ile lead thee through the wood,' sayd Robin;
'Good fellow, Ile be thy guide.'

'I seeke an outlawe,' the stranger sayd,
'Men call him Robin Hood;
Rather Ild meet with that proud outlawe
Than forty pound soe good.'

Robin Hood: The Spirit of the Forest

'Now come with me thou wighty yeman,
    And Robin thou soone shalt see:
But first let us some pastime find
    Under the greenwood tree.

'First let us some masterye make
    Among the woods so even,
Wee may chance to meet with Robin Hood
    Here att some unsett steven.'

They cutt them downe two summer shroggs,
    That grew both under a breere,
And sett them threescore rood in twaine
    To shoot the pricks y-fere.

Leade on, good fellowe,' wuoth Robin Hood,
    'Leade on I doe bidd thee.'
'Nay by my faith, good fellowe,' hee sayd,
    'My leader thou shalt bee.'

The first time Robin shot at the pricke,
    He mist but an inch it froe:
The yeoman he was an archer good,
    But he could never shoote soe.

The second shoote had the wighty yeman,
    He shote within the garlande,
But Robin he shott far better than hee,
    For he clave the good pricke wande.

'A blessing upon thy heart,' he sayd;
    'Good fellowe, thy shooting is goode;
For an thy hart be as good as thy hand,
    Thou wert better than Robin Hood.'

'Now tell me thy name, good fellowe,' sayd
        he,
    'Under the leaves of lyne.'
'Nay by my faith,' quoth bolde Robin,
    'Till thou have told me thine.'

'I dwell by dale and downe,' quoth hee,
    'And Robin to take Ime sworne;
And when I am called by my right name
    I am Guye of good Gisborne.'

Robin Hood: The Spirit of the Forest

'My dwelling is in this wood,' sayes Robin,
   'By thee I set right nought:
   I am Robin Hood of Barnesdale,
   Whom thou so long hast sought.'

He that had neither beene kithe nor kin,
   Might have seene a full fayre sight,
To see how together these yeomen went
   With blades both browne and bright.

To see how these yeomen together they
       fought
   Two howres of a summers day:
Yett neither Robin Hood nor Sir Guy
   Them fettled to flye away.

Robin was reachles on a roote,
   And stumbled at that tyde;
And Guy was quicke and nimble with-all,
   And hit him ore the left side.

"Ah, deare lady,' sayd Robin Hood, "thou
   That art both mother and may,'
I think it was never mans destinye
   To dye before his day.'

Robin thought on our ladye deere,
   And soone leapt up againe,
And strait he came with a backward stroke,
   And he Sir Guy hath slayne.

He took Sir Guy's head by the hayre,
   And sticked itt on his bowes end:
'Thou hast beene a traytor all thy liffe,
   Which thing must have an ende.'

Robin pulled forth an Irish kniffe,
   And nicked Sir Guy in the face,
That he was never on woman borne,
   Cold tell whose head it was.

Saies, 'Lye there, lye there, now Sir Guye,
   And with me be not wrothe;
If thou have had the worse strokes at my
       hande,
   Thou shalt have the better clothe.'

70

Robin Hood: The Spirit of the Forest

Robin did off his gowne of greene,
And on Sir Guye did it throwe,
And hee put on that capull hyde,
That cladd him topp to toe.

'Thy bowem thy arrowes, and litle horne,
Now with me I will beare;
For I will away to Barnesdale,
To To see how my men doe fayre.'

Robin Hood sett Guyes horne to his mouth,
And a loud blast in it did blow,
That beheard the sheriffe of Nottingham,
And he leaned under a lowe.

'Hearken, hearken,' said the sheriffe,
'I heare nowe tydings good,
For yonder I heare Sir Guy's horne blowe,
And he hath slaine Robin Hoode.

'Yonder I heare Sir Guye's horne blowe, Itt
blowes soe well in tyde,
And yonder comes that wighty yeoman,
Cladd in his capull hyde.

'Come hyther, come hyther, thou good Sir
Guy,
Aske what thou wilt of mee.'
'Oh I will none of ty gold,' sayd Robin,
'Nor I will none of thy fee:

'But now I've slaine the master,' he sayes,
Let me goe strike the knave;
This is all the rewarde I aske;
Nor noe other will I have.'

'Thou art a madman,' said the sheriffe,
'Thou sholdest have had a kight's fee:
But seeing thy asking hath beene soe bad,
Well granted it shale be.'

When Litle John heard his master speake,
  Well knewe he it was his steven:
'Now shall I be looset,' quoth Litle John,
  'With Christ his might in heaven.'

Fast Robin hee hyed him to Little John,
  He thought to loose him belive;
The sheriffe and all his companye
  Fast after him did drive.

'Stand abacke, stand abacke,' sayd Robin;
  'Why draw you mee soe neere?
Itt was never the use in our countrye,
  One's shrift another shold heere.'

But Robin pulled forth an Irish kniffe,
  And loosed John hand and foote,
And gave him Sir Guy's bow into his hand
  And bade it be his boote.

Then John he took Guye's bow in his hand,
  His bolts and arrowes each one:
When the sheriffe saw Little John bend his
      bow,
  He fettled him to be gone.

Towards his house in Nottingham towne
  He fled full fast away;
And so did all his companye:
  Not one behind wold stay.

But he cold neither runne soe fast,
  Nor away soe fast cold ryde,
But Litle John with an arrowe so broad
  He shott him into the syde.

This abrupt ending would be followed, no doubt, by fits of laughter on behalf of the audience! This is a good example of the ballad as an adventure story, but there are notable features of a more mystical nature.

The first is that the adventure is begun because of a dream, and none of the merry men, including John, are surprised that Robin should follow the vision. Moreover, the dream that he describes is not a clear portent of the future, for if anyone encounters and is bound by two 'wighty yemen' it is John, not Robin who conquers one alone.

The second element is Robin's call to the lady, not named as Mary, but described in quotation marks as both mother and may. This is clearly a pagan reference cloaked in Christian symbols, and perhaps it is even significant that John, who calls upon Christ, is captured until rescued by Robin. It is also clear that Robin is in trouble during the fight until he thinks of the lady, who gives him renewd strength, so great that he is able, after two hours of fighting, to behead Sir Guy with a single blow.

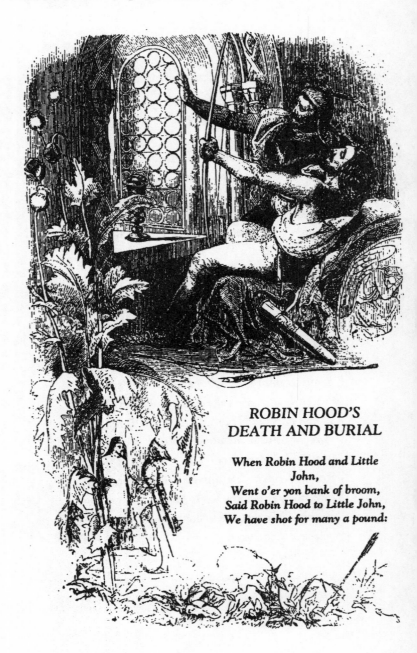

ROBIN HOOD'S DEATH AND BURIAL

When Robin Hood and Little
John,
Went o'er yon bank of broom,
Said Robin Hood to Little John,
We have shot for many a pound:

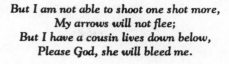

But I am not able to shoot one shot more,
My arrows will not flee;
But I have a cousin lives down below,
Please God, she will bleed me.

Now Robin is to fair Kirkley gone,
As fast as he can win;
But before he came there, as we do hear,
He was taken very ill.

And when that he came to fair Kirkley-
hall,
He knock'd all at the ring,
But none was so ready as his cousin
herself
For to let bold Robin in.

'Will you please to sit down, cousin
Robin,' she said,
'And drink some beer with me?'
'No, I will neither eat nor drink,
Till I am bled by thee,'

'Well, I have a room, cousin Robin,' she said,
'Which you did never see,
And if you please to walk therein,
You blooded by me shall be.'

She took him by the lilly-white hand,
And let him to a private room,
And there she blooded bold Robin Hood,
Whilst one drop of blood would run.

She blooded him in the vein of the arm,
And locked him up in the room;
There did he bleed all the live-long day,
Untill the next day at noon.

He then bethought him of a casement
door,
Thinking for to be gone,

Robin Hood: The Spirit of the Forest

*He was so weak he could not leap,
    Nor he could not get down.*

*He then bethought him of the bugle-
        horn,
    Which hung low to the knee,
    He set his horn unto his mouth,
    And blew out weak blasts three.*

*Then Little John, when hearing him,
    As he sat under the tree,
    'I fear my master is near dead,
        He blows so wearily.'*

*Then Little John to fair Kirkley is gone,
    As fast as he can dree;
    But when he came to Kirkley-hall,
    He broke locks two or three:*

*Untill he came bold Robin to,
    Then he fell on his knee;
    'A boon, a boon,' cries Little John,
        'Master, I beg of thee.'*

*'What is that boon,' quoth Robin Hood,
    'Little John, thou begs of me?'
    'It is to burn fair Kirkley Hall,
        And all their nunnery.'*

*'Now nay, now nay,' quoth Robin
        Hood,
    'That boon I'll not grant thee;
    I never "hurt" woman in all my life,
        Nor man in woman's company.*

*'I never hurt fair maid in all my time,
    Nor at the end shall it be;
    But give me my bent bow in my hand,
    And a broad arrow I'll let flee;
    And where this arrow is taken up,
    There shall my grave digg'd be.*

In this case the abrupt ending may be a collectors error, certainly the spelling, which is far more modern than in the other two ballads, suggests that is a copy of a copy. Other errors include rhyming 'ill' with 'win'. Nevertheless this is a fairly typical example of a good mediaeval death ballad, always a popular theme at a time when death lay so close to life.

One interesting point is that the Abbess is stated several times as being Robin's cousin, as if to emphasise the point. The Little Geste of Robin Hood describes her as 'The Pryoresse of Kykesley, that nye was of his kynne.' Perhaps some ancient controversy is reflected here.

The ballads of Robin Hood were only sparsely recorded, but a clear development can be seen, especially with the development of printing. By now one of the major themes of the early ballads had been lost, that of the devotion of Robin to the Virgin Mary. That this was a hearkening back to a time when Goddesses were as popular, if not more so, than Gods is very likely. What is more, it was the Minstrels who inherited the role of the Bards, and just as the Bards of the purely Celtic lands were the only ones able to keep the essence of Druidry alive after Christianity arrived, it naturally fell to the Minstrels to keep alive the native traditions of the English peasantry. With the gradual emancipation of those people, with the Reformation and English Renaissance, this aspect withered away and when printing began to spread Robin became predominantly a hero of adventures. Nobody asked about the Friar who kept company with them. Was he based upon the Culdee lay priesthood? Was Alan-A-Dale a symbol for the inner meaning of the entire minstrel tradition? We cannot say, but we can guess, speculate, and see the next stage in the growth of the legend of Robin. The advent of printing made many things possible, including the circulation of popular plays. Still in verse form, these following lines from "The Downfall of Robert, Earl of Huntingdon" by T. Heywood, were first published in 1601. They were found in the collection of David Garrick early in the last century, and are obviously only extracts, but they give an idea of what Robin had become by then.

Chorus ; Skelton the poet.

Skelton, (to the audience); 'The Youth that leads yon virgin by
the hand
As doth the Sun the Morning richly clad,
Is our Earl Robert-or your Robin Hood,
That in those days was Earl of Huntingdon.'

Robin Hood: The Spirit of the Forest

Robin recounts to Marian the pleasures of a forest life.

Robin: 'Marian, thou see'st tho' courtly pleasures want,
Yet country sport in Sherwood is not scant:
For the soul-ravishing delicious sound
Of instrumental music, we have found
The winged quiristers, with divers notes
Sent from their quaint recording pretty throats,
On every branch that compasseth our bower,
Without command contenting us each hour.
For arras hangings and rich tapestry,
We have sweet Nature's best embroidery.
For thy steel glass, wherein thou wont'st to look,
Thy chrystal eyes gaze in a chrystal brook.
At court a flower or two did deck thy head;
Now with whole garlands it is circled :
For what we want in wealth, we have in flowers;
And what we lose in halls, we find in bowers.'

Marian: "Marian hath all, sweet Robert, having thee;
And guesses thee as rich in having me.

Scarlet recounts to Scathlock the pleasures
of an outlaws life.

Scarlet: 'It's full seven years since we were outlaw'd first,
And wealthy Sherwood was our heritage.
For all those years we reigned uncontroll'd,
From Barnsdale shrogs to Nottingham's red cliffs.
At Blithe and Tickhill were we welcome guests;
Good George-a-green at Bradford was our friend
And wanton Wakefield's Pinner loved us well.
At Barnsley dwells a Potter tough and strong,
That never brook'd we brethren should have wrong.
The Nuns of Farnsfield, pretty Nuns they be,

Gave napkins, shirts, and bands, to him and me.
Bateman of Kendal gave us Kendal green,
And Sharpe of Leeds sharp arrows for us made.
At Rotherham dwelt our Bowyer, God him bless;
Jackson he hight, his bows did never miss.'

Fitzwater, banished, seeking his daughter
Matilda (Robin's Marian) in the forest of
Sherwood, makes his complaint.

Fitz: 'Well did he write, and mickle did he know,
That said "This world's felicity was woe'
Which greater states can hardly undergo."
Whilom Fitzwater in fair England's court
Possest felicity and happy state,
And in his hill blithe Fortune kept her sport;
Which glee one hour of woe did ruinate.
Fitzwater once had castles, towns and towers,
Fair gardens, orchards and delightful bowers;
But now nor garden, orchard, town, nor tower,
Hath poor Fitzwater left within his power.
Only wide walks are left me in the world,
Which these stiff limbs will hardly let me tread;
And when I sleep, heavn's glorious canopy
Me and my mossy couch doth overspread.'

He discovers Robin Hood sleeping;
Marian strewing flowers over him.

Fitz: " -in good time see where my comfort stands,
And by her lies dejected Huntingdon.
Look how my Flower holds flowers in her hands,
And flings those sweets upon my sleeping son.'

Robin Hood: The Spirit of the Forest

Feigns himself blind, to
see if she will know him.

Marian; 'What aged man art thou? or by what chance
Camest thou thus far into the wayless wood?'

Fitz: 'Widow, or wife, or maiden, if thou be;
Lend thee my hand: thou see'st cannot see.
Blessing betide thee! little feel'st thou want;
With me, good child, food is both hard and scant.
These smooth even veins assure me, He is kind,
Whatse'er he be, my girl, that thee doth find.
I poor and old am reft of all earth's good;
And desperately am crept into this wood,
To seek the poor man's patron, Robin Hood.'

Marian: 'And thou art welcome, welcome, aged man,
Aye ten times welcome to Maid Marian.
Here's wine to cheer thy heart; drink' aged man.
There's venison, and a knife; here's manchet fine.-
My Robin stirs, I must sing him asleep.

A judgement.
A Wicked Prior. Servingman.

Prior: 'What news with you, Sir?'
Serv.: 'Ev'n heavy news, my Lord; for the light fire,
Falling in manner of a fire-drake
Upon a barn of yours, has burnt six barns,
And not a strike of corn reserv'd from dust.
No hand could save it; yet ten thousand hands
Labour'd their best, though none for love of you:

For every tongue with bitter cursing bann'd
Your Lordship, as the viper of the land.'
Prior: "What meant the villains?'
Serv.: 'Thus and thus they cried;
"Upon this churl, this hoarder up of corn,
This spoiler of the Earl of Huntingdon,
This lust-defiled, merciless false Prior,
Heav'n raineth judgement down in shape of fire."
Old wives that scarce could with their crutches creep,
And little babes that newly earn'd t speak,
Men masterless that thorough want did weep,
All in one voice with a confused cry
In execrations bann'd you bitterly.
"Plague follow plague," they cried, "you have undone
The good Lord Robert, Earl of Huntingdon."

It's easy to see why Heywood never rivalled Shakespeare! Nevertheless, we can see certain features here. By this time Stukely has become Scathlock, shortly to become Scarlet. The death by fire is obviously quite different from the death scene now accepted in the myth, Robin has obviously died while sleeping in a barn. But the names and geography are very specific, and we can see that the Huntingdon story, rather than that of Robin of Locksley, had become the norm. And in this surviving extract we see the May flowers once again, reminding the urban audience of the greenwood and fields that they had left behind in the move to the city.

At first printing was reserved for what the rich considered to be important, but with the Civil War came a great demand for news, and this led to the proliferation of printing presses in the hands of those catering for a lower class of reader. This, and the emphasis on reading and interpreting the Bible for oneself that was central to Puritan Protestantism, led to the first great leap in rates of literacy. Of course, once people learnt to read the Bible alone was not enough and in order to cater for the new market the 18th Century saw the arrival of what were known as Chapbooks. These cheap and short pamphlets were sold by hawkers from town to town, in the same way that pots and pans and trinkets were peddled, and were the only ordinary literature available to the vast majority of people, especially those outside the larger towns. One or two firms only appear to to have been responsible for most of them, and they recounted popular tales from different parts of the country, of witches, legendary or real events, and of course stories of the great English heroes. They were also probably greatly responsible for keeping alive, and perhaps spreading the tales of Robin Hood, for he was always a popular Chapbook subject. These were prose renditions, and only recounted the basis of the story as we have it today, or individual incidents such as those covered in the earlier ballads, but they prepared the way for the next stage, which is largely represented by one man.

When printing became even simpler and cheaper at the end of the 18th Century, the time was right for the birth of the popular novel. We tend to think of writers such as Johnson, Defoe and the notorious John Cleland of Fanny Hill fame, but after a while this became an area in which middle class women were to excel, and for fifty or more years the most popular of novelists were such as Jane Austen and the Bronte sisters. But one man stood out as a writer of popular 'romances', as they were now now known, and it was Sir Walter Scott who first novelized Robin is his stirring adventure Ivanhoe. Here he recounted the version of the tale that has now become the standard.

The essential elements of the Robin story that Sir Walter incorporated came from many sources, and even if we can find most of the incidents in early work, it is difficult to know how much of the rest came from oral traditions which were still extant among the illiterate and poor, and how much was his own imagination. His own Scottish background leads to suggestions that separate legends, perhaps dating back to Robert The Bruce, had something to do with it. Yet here for the first time in a coherent form was the tale of Robin's loss of his inheritance, his encounter with Little John, the formation of the Merry Men, and above all the rescue of Marian, ending with the death scene.

It was Sir Walter who set the agenda for the future. But strangely enough, Robin now went into a temporary decline. Perhaps the strength of Scott's version put off the rest, for Robin now became mainly the province of the writers of stories for boys. While the Arthurian cycle was to see both an artistic revival via the pre-Raphaelite Brotherhood, and a mystical revival through such Golden Dawn members as A.E.Waite, Robin was left untouched.

The next phase of the development of Robin was from America. The development of the cinema led to massive demand for films, and every possible source was ransacked for stories, be they epics from the Bible, pirate tales, adventure novels or even, of course, the tale of Robin Hood. The Errol Flynn vehicle recounted the Walter Scott tale, although with pitched battles rather than cunning for the sake of spectacle, and the lack of a death scene for the sake of sequels. And sequels there were, far too numerous and usually far too awful to mention here. The theme was adventure, and the scene was a horrific Hollywood vision of Merrie England, with many a Hey Nonny No and a Fol De Rol Day. However, the next positive contribution to the Robin Hood saga also came from America, albeit as a result of one of its foulest moments.

With the advent of the 1950s, the Cold War and the nuclear threat came Senator Joseph McCarthy. His rabid condemnation of real and (mainly) imaginary communists was first aimed at the public services, but he found it was easier to gain publicity by aiming at Hollywood, a trick recently repeated by Dan Quayle with equal lack of success. The American public, it seems, were capable of being totally brain-washed into becoming God-hating Reds by the introduction of socialist themes into movies. Although McCarthy eventually became a figure of ridicule, largely due to the televising of his House Committee hearings. In the meantime, in a disgusting display of avaricious cowardice the studios buckled under and co-operated with the blacklisting of any scriptwriter with the mildest socialist leanings, one of whom lost his livelihood for donating a few dollars to a charity for Yugoslavian War Widows. But Hollywood's loss was Robin's gain, for at least one such writer fled to

England where, under an assumed name, he wrote many of the scripts for the British TV series, called simply The Adventures Of Robin Hood.

To most English people of my age the name of Robin Hood automatically conjures up a picture of Richard Greene in tights. I always remember him as a rather elderly Robin, but then the series did seem to run forever. The theme of this series was very much one of vengeance against the evil rulers, and perhaps of blacklisted writers against America and Sheriff McCarthy. The actors became so famous that few were able to get work elsewhere afterwards, and although the series was technically for children it became known to all and sundry. The theme song was so well known that recently a last-minute replacement Church Organist played it at a wedding, where the bride had requested the theme from "Robin Hood, Prince Of Thieves"!

Hollywood did put out a few more Robin films, and there were a couple of dire British attempts, ones that owed more to Hollywood than Sherwood. These hit the screens with a loud flop, but it was Richard Greene who ruled until usurped temporarily by a strangely significant Robin. This time he was a cartoon fox.

The 'Disney' version of Robin Hood was in fact made after the death of the great master of animation, and to a large extent was the second attempt to cash in on the enormous success of the final 'real' Disney cartoon, The Jungle Book. The figure of Little John was in every way, including voice, the same as Baloo the Bear, whose face and voice had been grafted onto an alley cat for the intervening film, The Aristocats. Nevertheless the cartoon Robin has something to be said for it. The choice of a Fox for Robin was a stroke of genius. It returned the idea of cunning and guile to Robin, adding the memories of Reynard, the great trickster of French fable, to the Robin Hood legend. It even repeated the transvestite theme in the opening sequence, when Robin and John hoodwink the Prince dressed as Gypsy fortune tellers. The film had Prince John and Richard as lions, one noble, the other mangey. It also repeated the concept, first seen in the Errol Flynn vehicle, of the miraculous appearance of Richard (in this case to reclaim the throne!), and of course avoided the death sequence, ending instead with a marriage. The film was firmly set in Merrie England, but at least the trees looked English, unlike the 'Star Wars' inspired pine forest of the Prince of Thieves, even if this Old English forest contained racoons.

Meanwhile, the success of the Richard Greene series had made Robin a target of satire. The Mel Brooks series 'When Things Were Rotten' made a very American assault on the legend, while Monty Python created a hybrid between Robin and Dick Turpin called 'Dennis Moore', played by John Cleese,that included a satire on the Richard Greene theme song (though not as rude as the one we sang at school). Cleese was to attack Robin again in Terry Gilliam's magnificent 'Time Bandits', in which a bunch of filthy (i.e. realistic) Merry Men are led by an immaculate pantomime Cleese. Even more recently, a children's comedy series made by the BBC, 'Maid Marian and Her Merry Men', gave a feminist slant to the story, with Marian as the real leader and Robin more concerned about cutting a dash at the Nottingham discos than with fighting the wicked Sheriff, played by the writer of the series, Tony Robinson, who had earlier been the henchman of the even more wicked Black Adder.

The presence in 'Time Bandits' of Sean Connery, as Agamemnon, leads us to the brilliant debunking of the commercial and romantic myth, the film 'Robin and Marian'. Here an older Robin, played by Sean Connery, who left England after a few run-ins with the Sheriff, has returned to England from the crusades a disillusioned man. With him comes Nicol Williamson as Little John. (Williamson was later to play an excellent Merlin in 'Excalibur'). He finds that Audrey Hepburn, as Marian, has, like Guinevere, become a nun, and that Alan-A-Dale has been scraping a living by recounting increasingly fantastic tales of their early adventures together. Forced by the popularity of the legend to play the part of the hero, he leads the peasants in a suicidal assault on the Normans and, when he is lying wounded after the defeat, is poisoned by Marian to avoid further pointless slaughter. It is a sad tale, but nevertheless an important reminder of the realities of the period for those blinded by Hollywood. It added to the legend by making Robin human, and the identification of Marian with the Abbess of Kirklees was revolutionary, but ultimately it detracted from the significance of Robin. It pointed out the anomalies in the historical aspect of Robin, but gave an entirely negative view of the role of epic myths. The legend of Robin Hood seemed set for another decline until the intervention of its greatest modern exponent, Richard Carpenter. After his 'Robin Of Sherwood' series things would never be the same again.

CHAPTER NINE

THE SON OF HERNE

WE have seen that the seemingly straightforward legend of Robin Hood has carried enormous mythological themes with it. It is, however, usually very difficult to determine the extent to which individuals performed the task of transmitting this esoteric material consciously. Early minstrels may have been aware of introducing themes from earlier tales, just as scriptwriters may have deliberately politicised or satirised Robin, but we rarely know exactly if or when that might have happened. No such problem exists with the television series 'Robin Of Sherwood'. For the first time since the early Bards began to transmit the secrets of Druidry through song, we have a writer who, quite deliberately and openly, emphasised and added to the inner traditions of Robin Hood, and that writer was Richard Carpenter.

The essential theme of Robin of Sherwood, be he Michael Praed or Jason Connery, Robin of Locksley or Robin of Huntingdon, became that Robin was the son of the mythical figure Herne The Hunter. Throughout the series Robin was called by the antlered figure of this ancient God, shrouded in mist, into the dark woods where wisdom and advice would be imparted to him.

The figure of Herne is, unfortunately perhaps, based upon a misconception. The legend of Herne is found mainly in association with Windsor Great Park, where he is said to be the ghost of a former gamekeeper. This is found in Shakespeare. Everywhere else Herne is in fact a Saxon hunting God whose name means Heron. The Heron is, of course, a fish-hunting bird, and the old God is particularly apposite for the islands of Britain. Surprisingly, the Heron as such does not feature in the Bird Ogham (see Appendix) although one letter is associated with the Cormorant. The antlered figure is based upon an earlier Celtic deity called Cernunnos. He is known only from a single inscription found in Paris, and this simply means 'horned', so Cernunnos may even be only a title rather than a proper God-name. The evidence of the Gundstrop cauldron seemed to fix him as a major deity, but this remarkable treasure, found in a Danish bog, his now been shown to be Thracian in origin. It shows distinct Indian influence, representing either Shiva, Orpheus, or both. His origin is in the antlered God Rudra, the original Shiva of the Hindu pantheon, who was worshipped by the Dravidians of Mohenjo-Daro and Harappa.

This should in no way detract from Carpenter's achievement. For the first time the archetypal aspect of Robin was brought to the attention of the public. It was incredibly daring given the fact that the vast majority of people still tend to associate any horned Gods with 'The devil'. However, Wiccan groups have long identified him with Pre-Christian fertility deities, realising correctly that the Christians only gave the Devil horns or antlers to insult and demean the earlier figures. This discovery was made by Professor Margaret Murray in the 1920s, and was turned into religious practise largely due to Gerald Gardner, the founder of the modern witchcraft movement.

Murray's research has now been largely discredited as histori-cally inaccurate, perhaps reflecting her wishes rather than her research. She claimed that the Witchcraft scares of mediaeval Europe and, later on, Scotland and England, reflected a genuine movement, itself descended from a prehistoric fertility cult. She believed that some of the confessions extracted from Inquisition victims were true, including tales of covens being headed by a 'Rabbin'. As I stated earlier, this probably reflects Catholic anti-semitism, suggesting that Jews were devil-worshippers, and indeed the word Rabbin was used until the last century as an anglicisation of Rabbi. Nevertheless, Murray found in these forced confessions, which in fact merely involved the victim agreeing with whatever fantasies the torturers spouted, the idea that Robin, with his band, were in fact a coven. As you will have seen by now, the tales of Robin Hood reflect just about every Pagan practice except for that of the supposed covens.

However, Murray was influential and her ideas at least began the interest in Pagan survivals in these islands. At around the same time Robert Graves, the poet, novelist and mythographer, intuited a cult of the triple-faced Moon Goddess as existing throughout Europe and the mediterranean. In many ways his work was as fallacious as Murray's, but it was inspirational in every sense, both in its formation and in its effect upon others, and amongst those others was Gerald Gardner, through whom Robin found his first modern religious expression.

Gardner began his movement in the early 1950s, and yet it was not the done thing to parade the horned God before the public, not surprisingly given the evil backlash that his honesty provoked. He nevertheless started a new religious movement based upon both the researches and imaginings of Murray and Graves and his contacts with some of those people who called themselves witches before he began his own work. As the new movement developed, Robin was incorporated, in the Murray sense, and as recently as the autumn of 1992 two modern witches, Nigel Bourne and Seldiy Bates, performed a brief ritual live on British Television in which Nigel took the role or at least the image, of Robin. Even with Gardner's work that would once have looked strange to a public seeing Robin as merely a figure of entertainment.

It was without doubt 'Robin Of Sherwood' that changed all that. Suddenly pagans began bringing him 'out of the closet', and every spiritual event became festooned with his image. The modern pagan Horned God has increasingly become associated with the Greenwood, and even if called Herne or Cernunnos, the relevant God here is truly Pan. The Ancient Greek lord of the Wildwood combined the fertility aspects with the fear of the untamed power of the forests, and his name recurs in the Robin legend in an unlikely way, as we shall see in the next chapter.

There was even more to Carpenter's achievement than this. By identifying Robin as the son of a God he elevated him, or perhaps restored him, to a status found nowadays only in India, where his relative Rama is worshipped still. Moreover, he introduced a large number of supernatural themes, making Robin the hero against whom the darkest powers, compared to which the Sheriff was just a sissy, could not prevail. He even restored the Arthurian link, found in the Ramayana and the legends of Gwynn Ap Nudd and Finn, in the'Seven Swords of Wayland', a feature-length special based upon the legendary Saxon smith-god who forged Excalibur.

The response to this series was overwhelming. Fan clubs sprang up which continue to this day, almost a decade after the original series ceased transmission. Like the 'Trekkies', who were able, after more than a decade, to gain a movie series of Star Trek and a new TV series to boot, they hope for more Robin Of Sherwood, and I for one will be overjoyed when it happens.

An interesting addition to this was the involvement of Mark Ryan, the actor who played Nazir. As mentioned in Chapter Seven this figure was thought to be an invention of Richard Carpenter's, but in fact harks back to the 'Moor' of the original Mayday celebrations. Mark became intensely involved in the symbolic aspects of the series, and went on to co-write the 100th edition of 'The Green Arrow', an American comic from the same stable as Superman and Batman whose hero is firmly based upon the Robin Hood imagery. It had the hero, who usually fires hi-tech arrows at super-villains, pay a visit to present-day Nottingham, where he dreams of a previous incarnation as Robin. In the course of his adventures he encounters the Goddess Elen, an ancient British deity rediscovered by Caroline Wise and Chesca Potter in the early 1980s, and the Black Alchemist, based upon a shadowy modern figure investigated by the same Andrew Collins who discovered the Robert the Bruce connection with Robin of Huntingdon.

The Robin Of Sherwood series has been, without doubt, the high point of the legend so far. If this seems blasphemy to medi-aevalists, just consider the fact that nowhere, in the ballads or the books, in films or TV, had the hidden Pagan legends that Robin inherited been specifically linked to him. Traditions are not just old things, they are living and continuous, and Carpenter brought Robin to a pinnacle. Of course, the film 'Robin Hood, Prince Of Thieves' has been very successful, but it had its tongue firmly in its cheek, introduced American accents into a forest of pine trees and otherwise rather spoiled things. A similar, British film released at the time sank more or less without trace.

The films, television series and even comics have added to the legend considerably. Their frequent refusal to deal with Robin's death have made him seem immortal, and the re-introduction of legendary themes have given Robin a new respectability. However, the last century has not only seen the development of the Robin Hood theme, it has also seen the rise of new heroes that can be shown to have been modelled upon him, and these are the subject of the next chapter.

CHAPTER TEN

THE SONS OF ROBIN

THE story of Robin has become so well known that it would have been highly unlikely not to influence more recent stories, though sometimes the connection is not obvious. At the end of the last century there were, as previously noted, a great deal of stories aimed at boys and based upon legendary heroes of Britain, such as Arthur, Robin, Hereward the Wake and so on. Particular writers seemed especially concerned to introduce mythical themes. One such was Rudyard Kipling, whose Puck of Pooks Hill placed the Robin Goodfellow archetype firmly in the Stone Age. His Jungle Book introduces Mowgli, the boy raised in the forest, and has many element taken from Jataka Tales (of the childhood of Buddha) that he learnt in India. Mowgli's contribution to the Robin legend will become obvious later, but the most obvious children's character to be based upon Robin is without doubt J.M.Barrie's Peter Pan.

Peter Pan has always been shown wearing a Robin Hood costume. This is never explained as such, it is merely assumed to be a childish disguise. His name once again links Robin with Pan, the Greek Lord of the Wildwood. The Never-Never Land of his adventures is an island of trees and coves, with the stuff of legends as its inhabitants. The theme of the story, of the innocence of childhood, harks back to a more relaxed time, destroyed by the advance of 'civilisation', and it was no surprise that Steven Spielberg, the prophet of (middle class American) childhood, decided to update the story in 'Hook'.

Peter Pan has become a major figure in the peculiar world of Pantomime. Originally an adult entertainment from Italy, Pantomime (the Pan- element here is more or less a co-incidence) has always revolved around sexual ambiguity; the same sense of strangeness tapped into by the transvestite shamans of many cultures and remembered in the man-Marian of the Morris dance. This means, of course, that Robin (!) Williams, in 'Hook', has become possibly the first man ever to play the part of Peter Pan, since in Pantomime the leading 'Boy' is always an actress, just as the dame or dames are actually actors. This strange tradition has been blindly accepted by the British, and it was left to English comedian Dick Emery, playing an Indian immigrant, to be shocked at hearing that his children were to be exposed to a play called Peter Pan starring a woman dressed as a man whose best friend is a fairy. Similar themes of cross-dressing are central to many folk-songs. This theme has continued, incidentally, in the only modern adult musical to reach Pantomime status, with audience participation throughout, The Rocky Horror Show. This seems to emphasise that the Pantomime theme is universal, since the audience-participation aspect developed not in the U.K. but in America, which has no pantomime tradition at all.

It is from America that we see the contribution of Robin to more modern legends even more clearly. A rather obvious example is that of the Prince in the Flash Gordon series. He dresses as Robin, has been dispossessed by the evil emperor, and lives in the woods with a band of rebels. This, however, is less an example of Robin's influence than a complete rip-off, and one that is always obvious to audiences. It deserved the treatment it got in the soft-porn comedy "Flesh Gordon", where the prince becomes a prancing queen.

The most famous and influential example of all is the story, first written in 1912, of an English nobleman, dispossessed of his heritage, who lives in the forest. He is an expert archer and defends the poor of his area from the ravages of evil outsiders. He strikes at them and then retreats into the forest, where they are unable to find him due to his expertise in the trees. He eventually rescues a beautiful woman who they have kidnapped, and takes her back into the forest to live as his wife. He is John Clayton IV, 8th Duke of Greystoke, better known as Tarzan of the Apes.

The story first appeared as a magazine 'pulp' series, and was called Tarzan the Apeman. It proved so popular that the series was novelized almost immediately as Tarzan Of The Apes. The writer, Edgar Rice Burroughs, was to all intents and purposes a hack author, capable of churning out an enormous volume of stories to strict deadlines. He was also a very good writer indeed. His narratie style is always pacey, and his stories, whether of Tarzan or the many other characters in his stable, such as John Carter of Mars, make excellent light reading. If it were not for the fact that he was indeed a hack, one would have to assume that he was some sort of professor of mythology, for in Tarzan he was able to recreate the essence of Robin, without, it would seem, any conscious intention. It has been suggested by Philip Jose Farmer, whose 'Tarzan Alive' is an excellent read as well, that the very pressure of the magazine deadlines made Burroughs, and the author of another hero he studied, 'Doc Savage', automatically discover legendary and mythic themes rather than going for 'originality'. These deadlines did not allow for much accuracy either; Tarzan's son was supposedly born in 1908, yet was able to fight in World War 1! Farmer does not note the similarity with Robin, but in a spoof genealogy of Tarzan he gives as an ancestor 'The Green Baron', an invented character supposedly the real model for Robin Hood.

Tarzan is, to a large extent, a mixture of Robin Hood and Mowgli. The first part of his name means White, linking him by co-incidence, though co-incidences seem to abound where Robin is concerned, with Finn MacCumhail and Gwynn Ap Nudd. The thirty-plus Tarzan books even include stories of the childhood of the hero, 'Tarzan's Jungle Tales'. These resemble those similar tales found about many legendary heroes and Gods, and of course Tarzan often gets elevated into a God by the various lost tribes and kingdoms that he discovers in the books, enough, according to one researcher, to fill the whole of Africa three times over. In these childhood stories he is very much a trickster figure, even stealing his first bow, a theme found in Shamanic initiations all over the world.

It took at least eight centuries for Robin Hood to make it to the silver screen, in the case of Tarzan it took just eight years, the Elmo Lincoln (!) version appearing in 1920, but the first really famous Tarzan was the Olympic champion swimmer Johnny Weismuller. He beat another Olympic swimmer to the role, Larry 'Buster' Crabbe, who was later to play Flash Gordon as well as Tarzan himself. The Weismuller vehicle unfortunately led to a degeneration of the character of Tarzan. In the original stories Tarzan can, after his first appearance, speak both English and French fluently, having taught himself to read English from the picture books he finds in his dead parents' hut; and he only lives in the jungle by choice, having given up the practical running of the Greystoke estate. The grunting image was finally lost in the TV series of Tarzan starring Ron Ely, where his archery skills were returned to him along with his education. Ron Ely went on to play Doc Savage, the subject of Philip Jose Farmer's other study in hack mythology. One of the effects of the powerful image of Tarzan was the creation of Africa, USA, an area made for film producers recreating the African flora and fauna, and this facility no doubt helped the proliferation of Tarzan films.

The original story of Tarzan has never really been filmed properly. One attempt was made, with Greystoke, The Legend Of Tarzan Of The Apes, which followed the advice of Tarzan Alive, making the so-called 'Great Apes' a little more human, but it was not faithful to either the Burroughs original or the Farmer development. Indeed, the scriptwriter was so disgusted with the final version that he demanded his name be removed from the credits and replaced with a pseudonym.

We cannot leave this area without looking at one recent updated but totally realistic version of the mythical theme represented both by Robin and the more recent Tarzan. As with 'Robin Of Sherwood', this was the work of someone who was quite aware of what he was doing, the person concerned being John Boorman, whose 'Excalibur' was a skilful examination of the Grail legends, far more so than any other film about Arthur. He created one of the most beautiful films I have ever seen, and unconsciously upated the Robin legend, in 'The Emerald Forest'. This story is based upon fact, but recreates the essential themes of Robin in a setting that is both modern and timeless. It tells of Tommy, the young son of an American engineer working on a dam project in Brazil, who is kidnapped by 'The Invisible People', a Lost Tribe. He grows up as son of the chief, who teaches him the art of archery as well as the way the tribe uses green stones to paint themselves in the colours of the forest, making themselves 'invisible'. Like Tarzan he rejects his inheritance when his real father arrives, but searches him out again when he has to defend the tribe from modern evil. Even after machine-guns have saved the day, he returns to the forest, taking the hearts and minds of the audience with him.

The Emerald Forest brings the story full-circle to its mesolithic origins. The shamanic dream-quests, the conjuring of rain to burst the dam that threatens their forest, all hark back to the primaeval forests of Britain as well as making a heartfelt plea for the forests of today, and their peoples, to be preserved. The final message, superimposed over a flying eagle, tells us that their are only 120,000 Indians left in the Amazon rainforests now, and that;

"They Remember What We Have Forgotten".

CHAPTER ELEVEN

THE GREEN MAN TODAY

THE figure of the Green Man is becoming increasingly important in a world sickened by the devastation caused by neglect of the Earth. The name comes from a series of carvings found again and again in old churches. These show a man both emerging from and part of foliage, a living spirit of the trees. Sometimes he emerges from the branches like Jack-in-the-green, in other carvings the foliage actually grows through his nose and mouth. It is only in modern times that he has been merged and named as one character.

He is not alone. The people who built old churches were not necessarily all Christians, indeed, conversion of the common people to Christianity was obtained by compulsion rather than conviction, so that the mandatory church attendance and true religious belief did not always go hand in hand. As the Roman church had always insisted upon churches being built over old Pagan sites, it became essential to those who still held to the old ways to keep the spot sacred to the old deities when the usage of such sites was changed. So old pagan deities were carved in inaccessible places, often out of sight, to laugh and grimace as the rougher elements at the back of the church indulged in their favourite hobby, according to outraged mediaeval church sources, of singing rude words to the hymns.

The Green Man was not Robin Hood, but they became the same. The Green Man inherited, through image, the role of Esus/ Osiris, emerging from the trees. He inherited the role of the Wild

Man, the Wodewose, still believed to inhabit the forests of Europe during the period, representing the raw, primaeval power of the forest, sacred to the 'little men' whose arrows were still feared.

This idea is still found today in Africa. The pygmies of the rainforests consider the forest, which for them is the same as the world, as a living spirit. These people are an ingenious lot, and their religious beliefs were unknown until fairly recently. In the past, in order to satisfy the preconceived notions of various anthropologists, they have stripped off their clothing for Victorian photographers wishing to show how primitive they were; invented a supreme God and rituals to go with it to satisfy other researchers, and even built bridges across rivers for Armand and Michaela Denis to film, even though they don't need them. However, their basic, deep animism is now clear. They don't need a name, or complicated rituals, to express their reverence for the forest, since it is constantly around them, part of their everyday experience.

This basic animistic feeling is shared by the neighbouring agricultural peoples too. There is a great tradition in West Africa of the Masquerade. This religious observance, ancestor of the great carnivals of Rio De Janciro, the West Indies and New Orleans, revolves around the adoption by the Masqueraders of various gods and goddesses through the wearing of particular masks and the performances of particular dances.

In those areas bordering the forest a fascinating and revealing Green Man masquerade is carried out once a year. A group of men go into the forest, and create an astonishing costume from the leaves of trees. One man wears this, and it makes him look like a dancing bus. He becomes possessed by the spirit of the forest. Returning to the village, he is enticed into the centre and then, as he dances, is placated by the villagers. He *is* the forest, as surely as is Robin. The entranced figure is a modern day Jack-in-the-Green, indeed the appearance is almost identical. I believe that an adaptation of this concept to the Robin myth is well overdue for performance in the 'civilised' world, where the power and beauty of the forest has been fatally neglected.

There is no doubt that Robin inherited his green clothing from this type of figure, symbolised by the Green Man carvings, just as he inherited stories and attributes from the various sources that I have already outlined. Had Christianity not eclipsed Paganism Robin would surely have been a God, and with the modern revival of interest in Paganism there is a new role for Robin to play.

It is not the little men of Europe's temperate rainforests who are in danger. They have left us long ago, by either extermination or by merging with the later peoples, but in the mighty tropical rainforests, the lungs of the world, their modern equivalents are battling for survival. In South America, where 20 million people once lived, only a few thousand remain. How one longs for the next bulldozer, logger or roadbuilder to run, screaming, from a wild, outlaw band and their arrows. Unfortunately the modern miners and loggers have more potent weapons than the Norman crossbow. And it is no longer merely the altars of forest sages that are being defiled, it is the entire planet.

The Greenwood represents the raw, primaeval forest from which all of our ancestors once emerged. Having outgrown our need for it as a habitat, we have learnt that we need it for the very air that we breathe, so that what was once condemned as mere sentiment is simple self-interest. The annual Mayday festival of new life symbolised the joy at greeting the inevitable return of fertility to the land, but now it has given way to a fear that life itself is in danger. We need a Robin. In fact, we need millions of Robins.

We need a new band of Merry Men, to defend the poor, and the Greenwoods upon which they depend. We can no longer look at the little men of the rainforests with civilised contempt, for it is not they, whose passage through the world vanishes so quickly, who are threatening the planet. We realise that they have retained what we have lost, and we seek to learn from their spiritual paths.

Yet we have our own traditions. Whether our ideal be Rama, Arthur or Horus, we recognise that if we let bad men rule the land, the land suffers and dies, and we must fight for good leaders, unless the concept of leadership itself has become so tainted as to need replacement. The legends of the past can inspire us, lead us away from self-destruction towards a new relationship with our world. But we have to become our own heroes, to inspire our own legends.

A fascinating attempt at something of the sort was attempted by the esotericist John Hargrave in the 1920s and 1930s, and I am indebted to Terry Baker for his ground-breaking research into this unjustly forgotten figure. Hargrave led an adult break-away from the Boy Scout ovement, in which he had once been a prominent member. This was known as the Kibbo Kift Kindred, Kibbo Kift being old country slang for an upright, dependable fellow. They were interested in the Greenwood, the Shamans associated with the older, natural way of living (long before Mircea Eliade, let alone Kenneth Meadows, were to popularise the concept), and wore a green Saxon-style jerkin complete with hood. Instead of Jamborees they held four moots, on the dates of the four major Celtic festivls. He later attempted to make this into a political movement, the Social Credit Party or Greenshirts. Unlike certain German equivalents in the Volkische groups he refused to have anything to do with the Fascist perversion and his movement, once ten thousand strong, withered away, except in Canada, where the SCP held power in one state from the end of the Second World War until 1983, the year of his death. Unfortunately they were unable to implement the more radical aspects of Social Credit theory due to the nature of Canada's constitution. In Britain the high-point of their notoriety came in 1940, when a member fired an arrow with Social Credit slogans (including 'End Hitlerism') through the open door of No.10 Downing Street. The press dubbed this man 'The Robin Hood Of Downing Street'. His name, strangely enough, was R.J.Green. Nevertheless, a break-away section that wanted to leave the politics alone became the Woodcraft Folk, who, as a less jingoistic alternative to the Scout movement, are currently undergoing a massive revival, with Socialist and Ecologically-minded parents sending their children along. The Kibbo Kift were certainly the first Green movement, and Robin would have been proud of them.

I firmly believe that spiritual work with the earth and its life is important, but I am equally sure that spiritual work alone is not enough. As we abandon the sterile death-cults that have turned our eyes towards starry heavens and imagined hells while the ground beneath our feet is poisoned, and learnt to distrust the money-cults that have led to the poisoning, it is not enough to close our eyes and dream of different paths. The path through the Greenwood is a real path, not one simply to be imagined.

With regards spiritual exercises, there are many practical ways to get into contact with the spirit of the woods. The most obvious place is with the trees. Trees have long had a special significance in esoteric lore. Apart from the tree of Yggdrasil and that from which Osiris/Esus emerged, there is the Otz Chiim, the Tree Of Life of the Cabala, there are Sufi equivalents, and to this day the sacred drummers of Nigeria know that they must pray to a tree before cutting it down to use it for a drum.

Find a tree in a fairly secluded spot that you feel some attraction for. First, sit in front of it, facing it. With your eyes, follow the growth of the tree from the moment that it emerges from the ground to it very tips. When you have done this go back down to its first branches. Follow the spread of the branch to its end, then go back. Take your time with this. Even with a small tree this process should take a quarter of an hour, and you should not feel worried about choosing one that will take an entire hour. Do not skip from the edge of one branch to another, always travel back to the point where the two diverge. It is up to you how detailed you should make this process, obviously you will have the chance to do this again, and when you do so, find another spot from which to view the tree. In time this tree will feel as familiar as an age-old friend, which indeed it is.

The second stage consists of sitting with your back to the tree, but not leaning on it yet, looking out over the spot where you were sitting before. Follow the spread of the ground away from you, spotting where different trees, plants and stones come into view. If you spot an animal, watch it until it goes out of sight. Always be aware that the roots of the tree are beneath you, spreading out underneath much of what you see. Again, on future occasions find a different angle away from the tree, so that eventually you are as aware of the environment within which it stands as you are of the tree itself. Note which plants grow close to it, for the chances are that they depend upon it in some way. A tree is an entire ecosystem, playing host to many species and providing food and moisture to many more, both animal and vegetable.

Finally, for the third stage stand with your back to the tree, leaning upon it. Feel your spine as part of the tree, feel your feet sinking towards the earth, with your toes as rootlets. Let your arms rise as branches and your fingers become twigs.

If it is possible, you can also sleep beneath the tree, in which case your dreams should also be of great interest! Also, especially in springtime, find a stethoscope and listen to the heartbeat of the tree, for it really has one. As the sap rises, you will learn a sound to remember in the third stage as you become at one with the tree.

Do not feel afraid to accept gifts from the tree in the form of nuts or fruit. It is tempting and sentimental to consider these the property of birds and small mammals, but we must remember that we are part of nature too. If you choose a member of the Pine family you may also find resin for use in incenses, and twigs that have fallen from the tree as a natural part of its growth can be used for sacred fires, though be careful not to damage the tree itself!

Next, find out about that tree. What is its species, its modern name. Also, who was it sacred to? You will find, whether in Britain or America or anywhere else, that there is ancient lore concerning that species. It may be part of the Bardic Tree Alphabet (see Appendix) in which case it will have a specific letter, and will have been considered to be linked to certain birds, animals etc. It may have had specific uses in the past that gave it great value, whether for fencing, basket-weaving, walking-sticks, arrows, church-gates or even cricket bats! Not all such crafts have died out, in which case you may be able to learn, and even do, a great deal. Try to estimate its age, for in some cases it may well date back to a time when such things were not forgotten.

This personal way of uniting with the Greenwood is good, but in our modern world it is not enough. To truly serve the spirit of the Greenwood we must be prepared to take part in the necessary social and political action to save our trees.

Once, as we have seen, we were able to live in harmony with the Greenwood. We could even cut it down to make homes and tools without having a permanent effect upon it, since we took so little and it grew so swiftly. That time has gone.

Recently in England many of those involved in a variety of Esoteric and Pagan paths have united to fight a proposed motorway that threatens to destroy London's last remaining stretch of ancient woodland, hitherto untouched since it began growing after the last Ice Age. This is Oxleas Wood, where once the King of England and his Queen, along with the Guilds of the City Of London, once watched Marian and Robin at their Mayday Revels. At the time of writing this battle has yet to be won, though it is by no means lost. There are hundreds of such battles to be fought. We need millions of merry men and women to fight the servants of evil powers, and if 'evil' seems a bit strong, the wickedness of Prince John and his Sheriff never approached that of those modern powers in destroying and oppressing native peoples and appropriating their rights to the forests. By involving ourselves in these battles we can let the spirit of Robin and his band live on in ourselves.

One such fight has already been inspired by Robin, in the form of an organisation called 'Robin's Greenwood Gang'. This was formed in the early 1980s at Stonehenge, when there was still a large Midsummer festival held there each year. Unfortunately, some people who came more for the music than for any other reason were extremely uncaring of the environment. Everyone used to love sitting around a fire in the evening, but the wood provided by the organisers soon ran out and some people began hacking down trees. The Greenwood Gang was set up to stop this by peaceful means, mainly a question of persuading the people concerned that green wood simply doesn't burn. Since then they have gone on to become an active grassroots movement, and their address, along with that of other relevant organisations, is given at the end of the book.

We must be prepared to become 'extremists', or at least take extreme attitudes, towards protecting our woods. It is all very well to allow the 'farming' of trees in managed plantations, to provide wood for paper and furniture, but we must not allow the wholesale devastation that is taking place in such places as Canada and California. Nor must we allow the importations of tropical hardwoods, for no matter how unsightly pine furniture may be, at least it is not being cut at the expense of native peoples whose way of life is so harmless compared to our own. However, we must also fight to save temperate broadleaf rainforests from being replaced by 'plantations' that cannot support the native ecology, such as is happening in Scotland. There is beautiful wooden furniture to be found, let the slogan be 'second-hand is better than new'!

We cannot compromise any more. Each clump of trees is special now. We have traded the beauty and seclusion of woodland for housing and industry, farming and transport. Now that we have declining mass-manufacture, excess food stocks, thousands of empty houses awaiting repair and massive air pollution from the motor car we must fight for every last tree. We have no need of yet another road or housing estate, but we now know scientifically what our ancestors knew from practical experience and instinctive reverence, we need our woods and forests.

Robin has, through the recent spiritualised version of Richard Carpenter, taken on a significance denied for a millenium. The Horned Man, common in Wiccan circles and now found throughout the Pagan and Neopagan movements, is more than ever depicted in the Greenwood as a nature God rather than a purely 'fertility' deity. The interest in the Green man figure that has grown up since the Green movement began growing can lead us to a new appreciation of the spirit of the forest.

Robin, like Arthur, must come again, and we must be prepared, each of us, to declare that he is here, he is angry, he is still fighting, and he is us.

APPENDIX 1

THE BARDIC TREE ALPHABET

MANY early alphabets had names for their letters, and this was true for the Gaelic alphabet, devised in the Mediaeval period for the writing of Classical Gaelic, the literary language of the courts of Ireland, Scotland and Man. The lore associated with the tree-names used for the writing of this alphabet is far older. The Bards, both in Gaelic and Brythonic Celtdom, were the last to be suppressed, indeed the schools in Ireland survived until Cromwell. It was thus possible to use this alphabet to record the tree-lore that was once common to the entire Celtic Druid tradition, including that which was once common in England.

This alphabet was an adaptation of the Roman alphabet to fit an earlier system, that of Ogham. There were two forms of this alphabet, the straight-line Ogham of most stone monuments and the branch Ogham, so called because the letters looked like trees. A similar system of branch-Runes existed. Ogham fought a long and unsuccessful battle against the Roman script, but in Ireland at least the old lore was incorporated into the new writing, and this also happened in Wales, which had experienced widespread Irish immigration at the beginning of the Christian era. When Robert Graves introduced this system to a wide audience in 'The White Goddess' he was accused by some critics of having made it up! Yet, ten years later, a priest writing an introduction to an Irish Gaelic primer lamented the fact that the old names for the letters were falling into disuse, a strange way to describe a tradition only a decade old!

Robin Hood became the inheritor of the sacred feelings we once had for our trees, feelings that were investigated and codified by the Druids, who were the heirs to a tradition older than the stone circles of Britain. In the modern esoteric world there is much argument, often based upon lamentable racial prejudice, about which system is 'best' for English. The tree alphabet surely wins this argument against Hebrew, Runes and the like, simply because it is closest to our Latin Alphabet and links in with the fullness of the British tradition, which has been the property of many races and has now, for better or worse, become that of much of the modern world. Through it, and the correspondences, we can rediscover what our ancestors felt about the trees and nature in general, helping us to re-establish a valuable tradition that is of vital importance if we are to regain our spiritual link with the Greenwood.

Letter	Name	Tree	Bird	Number	Month	Colour
B	Bet	Birch	Pheasant	5	24/12-20/1	White
L	Luis	Rowan	Duck	14	21/1-17/2	Grey
F	Fearn	Alder	Seagull	8	18/3-14/4	Crimson
S	Saille	White Willow	Hawk	16	15/4-12/5	Brightness
N	Nuin	Black Ash	Snipe	13	18/2-17/3	Clearness
H	Huath	Hawthorn	Night-Crow	0	13/5-9/6	Purple
D	Duir	Oak	Wren	12	10/6-7/7	Black
T	Tinne	Holly	Starling	11	8/7-6/8	Grey-Green
K	Coll	Hazel	Crane	9	5/8-1/9	Nut Brown
Qu	Quert	Crabapple	Hen	-	as Coll	Apple-Green
M	Muin	Thorn	Titmouse	6	2/9-29/9	Variegated
G	Gort	Ivy	Mute Swan	10	30/9-27/10	Blue
Ng	Ngetal	Reed	Goose	1	28/10-24/11	Clear Green
St	Straif	Sloe	Thrush	-	as Ruis	Purple-Black
R	Ruis	Elder	Rook	-	25/11-22/12	Tawny Red
A	Ailm	Elm	Lapwing	-	-	Black & White
O	Ohn	Furze	Cormorant	-	-	Saffron
U	Ur	Heather	Skylark	-	-	Light Green
E	Eadha	Aspen	Whistling Swan	-	-	Light Yellow
I	Ioho	Yew	Eaglet	-	-	Dark Brown

This alphabet acted as a system for memorising Bardic Lore. In the original Gaelic, the names of the birds usually begin with the same letter as the tree and, of course, the letter itself. As with most ancient alphabets the letters are named, but in this case entirely for trees (the Hebrew letters, for example, are named after aspects of pastoral life such as Oxen, Fences etc.).

The Druids controlled the cutting down of trees, and unauthorised felling was punishable by fines or, in the case of a 'prayer tree', by death. These trees, still found in Ireland, had cloth tied to the branches, each representing a prayer or a wish, and this is still remembered in tree-dressing ceremonies in England.

By tying in observation in the woods with the calendar it is possible to watch the living cycle of the year, expressed in the trees themselves, and in a manner going back thousands of years. You can add to this calendar by wearing the appropriate colour in the woods, although 'brightness' may be a problem!

Appendix 2

Relevant groups and publications

Select Bibliography

The Ramayana
The Mahabharata
Book of Days 1878
Aswynn, Freya, **Leaves of Yggdrasil**, London 1988
Ash, Geoffrey, **King Arthur**, London 1990
Barrie, J M, **Peter Pan**
Book of Ballads, London 1820
Burroughs, Edgar Rice, **Tarzan of the Apes**, many editions
Davidson, H R, **Gods and Myths of Northern Europe** London 1964
Ebbutt, M I, **Myths and Legends of the British**, London 18—
Eliade, Mircea, **The Myth of the Eternal Return** Princeton 1971
Eliade, Mircea, **Shamanism, Archaic Techniques of Ecstacy,**
Princeton 1964
Farmer, Philip Jose, **Tarzan Alive**
Graves, Robert, **The White Goddess,** London 1959
Guest, C, **The Mabinogion**, (Llanerch edition) 1990
Hartzell, Hal, **The Yew Tree, A Thousand Whispers**, Oregon 1991
Heath-Stubbs, John, **The Mythology of Falstaff**, The Occult
Observer No 1, 1949
Larry, Lucie, **Egyptian Mysteries** London 1981
Machen, Arthur, **The Bowmen and Other Legends of the War**
London 1915
Merrie England - A Book of Plays, London 18—

Murray, Colin and Liz, **The Celtic Tree Oracle**
Murray, Margaret, **The God of the Witches London** 1962
Mackenzie, Donald, **Indian Myths and Legends,** London 18—
Nichols, Ross, **The Book of Druidry,** London 1990
Pennick, Nigel, **Practical Magic in the Northern Tradition,** London 1989
Pennick, Nigel, **Lines on the Landscape,** London 1989
Pennick, Nigel, **The Celtic Oracle,** London 1991
Pennick, Nigel, **The Secret Lore of Runes and Other Alphabets** London 1991
Potter C, and Wise, C, **Elen, Guardian of the Shimmering Ways,** Oxford 1985
Robinson, John J, **Born In Blood,** London 1990
Robertson, Olivia, **The Fellowship of Isis Handbook** Clonegal 1992
Robertson, Olivia, **The Rite of Dana, Druid Initiation,** Clonegal 1992
Rollinson, **Myths and Legends of the Celtic Race,** London 1911
White, T H, **The Once and Future King**

Useful Addresses

for the religion of the Goddess and the Druid Clan of Dana
The Fellowship of Isis
Foundation Centre
Clonegal Castle
Enniscorthy
Eire

The Council of British Druid Orders
125 Magyar Crescent
Nuneaton
Warcs
CV11 4SJ

On Target
Spirit of Sherwood magazine
1276 West Marshall
Ferndale
Michigan
48220
USA

Robin's Greenwood Gang
96 Church Road
Readfield
Bristol 5

Dragon (Don't Ruin Anything Green or Natural)
c/o P O Box 196
London WC1A 2DY
(For details of how you can help Oxleas Wood)

Index

A

Abbots Bromley Horn Dance   28
Africa   8, 11, 56
African   9, 13
Agincourt   41, 42
Agnar   24, 26, 27, 32
Alan-A-Dale   35, 78, 86
Alps   11
Amazon   12
America   84, 85, 94
American   2, 45, 92
Anglo-Norman   26, 29, 53
Anglo-Saxon   25, 31
Anglo-Saxonism   3
Animism   99
Arrow   17
Arthur   2, 3, 15, 16, 17, 19, 31, 32, 34, 35, 39, 55, 84, 93, 97, 100, 106
Arthuri   55
Arthurian   14, 31, 91
Austrians   40
Avalon   16
Avebury   9
Ayodhya   14

B

Baal   26
Babel   17
Baker, Terry   101
Bardic   35
Bardic Tree Alphabet   103
Bards   13, 32, 35, 78, 88
Basque   6
Battle of Mons   42
Belgium   26
Bermondsey   22, 23
Bhakti   13
Blackheath   23
Blondel   23
Bourne, Nigel and Bates, Seldiy   90

Bow   15, 17, 40, 41, 96
Bowshot   43, 45
Brahmanism   26
Brazil   97
Breton   6
Britain   8, 9, 10, 11, 12, 20, 21, 25
British   33, 42, 92
British Isles   7
Bronze   12
Bronze Age   8, 10, 11
Brooks, Mel   86
Buddha   17
Buddhist   26
Burroughs, Edgar Rice   95
Bushmen   8

C

Cabala   102
Canada   7, 101
Carpenter, Richard   52, 87, 88, 89, 91, 105
Catal Huyuk   8
Caucasus   5
Celtic   6, 7, 10, 12, 14, 21, 25, 26, 27, 29, 31, 32, 33, 35, 46, 58, 78, 101
Celtic scholars   34
Celts   5, 6, 7, 8, 12, 25, 26, 46
Cernunnos   89, 90
Cerridwen   22, 58
Ceylon   15
Chapbook   83
Chapbooks   82
Charlemagne   13
Charles   55
Charles II   21, 55
Charlton   22, 23, 51, 58
Charlton House   22
Chesca Potter   91
Christ   14
Christian   16, 26
Christianity   6, 13, 25, 27, 29, 31, 78,

Mahabharata 13, 14
Mahatma Gandhi 16
Maid 52
Maid Marian 1, 47, 49, 50
Maid Marian and Her Merry Men 86
Malaya 8
Manx 6
Marian 15, 16, 32, 50, 51, 54, 56, 83, 86, 87, 104
Marmar 28
Mars 20
Masquerade 99
May 49, 52, 82
Maya 16
Mayday 3, 32, 33, 35, 41, 42, 45, 46, 55, 56, 100, 104
Maypole 47, 51, 56
Maypoles 46
McCarthy, Joseph 84
Meadows, Keneth 101
Melvas 55
Merlin 15, 86
Merry Men 40, 83, 86
Merry Men, 100
Mesolithic 7, 8, 9, 10, 29, 42, 44, 97
Mesoliths 12
Minstrels 35, 58, 78, 88
Mohenjo-Dara 15
Mohenjo-Daro 89
Mons 42, 43
Morgan-Le-Fay 16
Morris 3, 46, 51, 53, 54
Morris dance 51, 94
Morris dancing 28, 53
Mowgli 93, 95
Murray, Margaret 29, 89

N

Native American 45
Native Americans 8
Nazir 53, 91
Ndo-Europeans 26
Neolithic 6, 7, 8, 9, 10, 12, 43, 44
Neoliths 9, 11
New Grange 7, 9
New Guinea 10
Nichols, Ross 55

Nimrod 17
Norman 1, 25, 33, 39, 58, 100
Normans 3, 27, 40, 86
Norns 27
Nottingham 86, 91

O

Oak 21, 23
Occult Review 43
Odin 26, 27, 28, 29, 31, 32, 33
Odinic 29
Odinism 26, 27, 29
Ogham 27, 89
Old Sarum 44
One tree' hills 46
Order Of Bards, Ovates and Druids 55
Orpheus 89
Osiris 20, 21, 23, 24, 33, 99, 102
Ossian 35, 38, 39
Ossianic 39
Oxleas Wood 51, 104

P

Pagan 25, 27, 28, 49, 54, 58, 90, 92, 98, 104, 105
Paganism 29, 100
Pagans 33, 90
Pan 90, 93
Pantomime 94
Peasant 40
Peasantry 78
Peasants' Revolt 1
Pelagian 58
Persephone 33
Persia 3
Persian 33
Persians 5
Peter Pan 93, 94
Pharaoh 20
Philip Jose Farmer 95
Potter, Chesca 91
Pre-Raphaelite Brotherhood 84
Puck 59, 93
Pygmies 9
pygmies 99
Queen of May 49

'The Robin Hood Of Downing Street' 101
The Rocky Horror Show   94
Thor   26
Thracian   89
Time Bandits   51, 86
Tir Na nOg   38
Trojan Wars   13
Troubadour   58
Troubadours   35, 58
Turkey   3, 8, 13
Turkish   20

U

Underworld   32, 33
Upanishads   13–31
Uther Pendragon   15

V

Vedas   13, 15
Vikings   25, 26
Virgin Mary   58, 78
Vishnu   13, 14, 15, 16

W

Waite, A E   84
Wales   12, 25, 33, 58
Welsh   6, 11, 31, 32, 40, 42
White   33
Whitsun   46
Wiccan   89, 105
Wild   33
Wild Hunt   33
Wildwood   7, 91, 93
Will Scarlet   57
William Tell   40
Williamson, Nicol   86
Windsor Great Park   88
Wise, Caroline   91
Witchcraft   1, 29, 89
Woden   26
Woodcraft Folk   101
Woolwich   22
Worcestershire   40
Wotan   26

Y

Yggdrasil   27, 102

Z

Zeus   26

117